HAUNTED
LEICESTER

HAUNTED
LEICESTER

ANDREW JAMES WRIGHT

TEMPUS

Frontispiece: *A rather eerie example of stonework on a tomb in Welford Road Cemetery.*

First published 2005

Tempus Publishing Limited
The Mill, Brimscombe Port,
Stroud, Gloucestershire, GL5 2QG
www.tempus-publishing.com

British Library Cataloguing in Publication Data.
A catalogue record for this book is available from the British Library.

ISBN 0 7524 3746 1

Typesetting and origination by Tempus Publishing Limited.
Printed in Great Britain.

CONTENTS

ACKNOWLEDGEMENTS

I would like to thank the following people: Keith Bindley, David Paul Booth, James Bowie, Mike Brearey, Fred Clarke, Trevor Edwards, Dave Flanagan, Norman Gambin, Dorian and Kim Gamble, Dr Alan Gauld, Norman and Maureen Green, Maurice Grosse, Brian Johnson, Linda Kelly, Susan Mc Lean, Frank Maunder, Bill Melia, Robert Salmon, Sharon Smith, Tom Smith, Daena Smoller, Barry Spencer, Malc Tovey, Arthur David Warner, Val Weafer, Tony Webster.

ABOUT THE AUTHOR

Andrew James Wright was born in Leicester in 1955. He has worked in the family business, a pub, had a spell in the retail trade, the record industry, been employed as a carpenter and is presently part of the estates team at the University of Leicester. A frustrated poet and keen cartoonist, he also enjoys fishing, gardening and keeping ferrets. He has been consulted widely on the subject of ghosts and regularly gives talks on the subject.

INTRODUCTION

Leicester – or *Ratae Coritanorum*, as the Romans called the town – started as a Celtic settlement. The Romans invaded England in AD 43 and took Leicestershire in AD 47. With their ingenuity they built roads, drains and a forum in the centre where goods would be exchanged or purchased. Also, a temple was built on the area now known as St Nicholas Circle.

During the Middle Ages leather and wood were the main requirement. An annual fair was held which enabled the buying and selling of various produce. There was also a weekly market for supplies of crops, meat and other necessities.

In 1800 the population of Leicester would have been around 17,000. The Leicester Royal Infirmary was established at this time and a section of canal was navigated from the River Soar on which barges would bring in coal and iron to the city. Other modernisation such as a sewer system and gas lighting would follow as the Industrial Revolution began in earnest. With its hosiery firms and shoe manufacture, the city would prosper.

Today Leicester is a typical modern city. It boasts one of the largest markets in Europe, two universities, a racecourse, a multitude of museums and a fine art gallery. The city is a 'shopper's paradise' with the huge Shires Shopping Centre, the Castle Park and Lanes areas with a colourful variety of designer shops bringing a cosmopolitan flavour and the seemingly endless array of pubs, bars, cafes and restaurants to suit all styles and tastes.

But, there may be a darker, mysterious side. There are quiet little avenues, winding, cobbled streets with imposing-looking buildings. As darkness sets in, these quiet places, to some, can be most disconcerting. Perhaps an oppressive atmosphere, almost surreal, a scent of out-of-season lavender, a shadow moving swiftly, caught in peripheral vision. Ghosts perhaps?

The population of Leicester is now nearly 280,000. Judging by the number of well-attended 'Ghost Walks' and related events there must surely be a sizeable population of phantoms in the city as well.

Let us now explore the ghostly heritage of Leicester.

Overleaf: *St Mary de Castro; several strange occurrences have been experienced here.*

ONE

THE OLD TOWN

The Blue Boar Inn

Whenever the subject of ghosts comes up in conversation, the Blue Boar will inevitably pop up. Although the inn and its ghost have long since gone, it is one of those tales that gets passed down through the generations.

The Blue Boar Inn stood on the old High Street, which today is part of Highcross Street, opposite Freeschool Lane. In medieval times it was called Dead Lane. The inn was originally called the White Boar. Richard III stayed there on the eve of the Battle of Bosworth, which took place on 22 August 1485. Travelling in fine style, on his journey he even brought his own bed. This he left at the inn certain to reclaim it after his victory over Henry Tudor.

As a result of the King losing his life and the battle, the inn became the Blue Boar. The emblem of a white boar was the badge of Richard III so it seemed prudent to change it to that of the Earl of Oxford, he being a supporter of Henry Tudor. The bed itself remained at the inn, passing from landlord to landlord.

In the early sixteenth century a cache of gold coins were discovered in a false bottom of the bed by the then landlord, Thomas Clarke. The cache amounted to £300, which in those days was a huge fortune. He tried to keep the matter secret but of course in a pub environment with gossip and rumour rife, the word eventually got out. The Clarkes did very well and Thomas later became a Lord Mayor.

After Thomas Clarke's death, his widow Agnes ran the inn. A man called Harrison, who had heard of the fortune, stayed at the inn and worked his charm on the chambermaid, Alice Grumbold. He learned that Agnes Clarke would be no easy target. She was a fearsome woman! There was no room for the meek running a town inn in those days. She would have stood between many a brawling man and thrown a good few out on their ear. Harrison rounded up some hefty men and with Alice Grumbold hatched a plan to rob the inn and leave Leicester. A few days later, the robbery took place.

Agnes tried bravely to defend herself but was easily overpowered by the seven rogues who were intent on taking whatever gold remained. One man called Bradshaw tried to silence Agnes from screaming by thrusting his fingers down Agnes's throat. As a result she choked to death. Not long after, the robbers and the chambermaid were rounded up. Bradshaw was hanged and Alice Grumbold was burnt at the stake.

Claims from residents and customers of a whitish apparition began to circulate. The thing would apparently glide silently about the place on frequent occasions. The phantom was of course assumed to be that of Agnes Clarke. The sightings continued until the inn was demolished in 1836.

A new Blue Boar Inn opened in the same year. It was situated on Southgate Street opposite Friar Lane. It became a very popular pub. Many customers claimed that the shade of Agnes

The Blue Boar, where the murder of Agnes Clarke resulted in her haunting the pub.

Clarke haunted this inn also. The Blue Boar was set for demolition in the mid-1960s in order for major redevelopment of the area. Shortly before the pub was pulled down, an inquisitive beat bobby was pelted with stones while in the deserted building. The bed that Richard III left behind was taken to Beaumanor Hall near Woodhouse Eaves, a village some eight miles north-west of Leicester.

In the Recorder's Bedroom at Leicester Guildhall there was a bed that, at one time, according to legend, came from Beaumanor Hall. Some believe this was the same bed that eventually led to the murder of Agnes Clarke. In recent years there have been sightings of a ghost called 'the White Lady'. Is this the restless ghost of Agnes Clarke?

St Martin's Cathedral

The 220ft spire of St Martin's Cathedral has dominated the Leicester skyline since the eighteenth century, even today it still has superiority in height, as modern buildings reach ever higher. The cathedral is certainly not as grand as those of Ely or Lincoln but it does have its beauty and charm.

St Martin of Tours (AD 316-97) was a converted Roman soldier, a holy man and a humanitarian, who became the city's patron saint. There are a number of features within the cathedral depicting this kind and gentle man. At the North Door there exists a small statue that looks down on those entering. In St George's Chapel, where the Leicestershire Regiment have their memorial chapel, is a rather splendid depiction in the south-west window. Three saints are seen here portrayed as examples to soldiers: St George to remind them of their loyalty to England, St Alban to remind them that it is noble to die for what is right and St Martin to remind them that he cares for them. St Martin is carved into St Dunstan's Altar, which reflects the work inspired by Martin. St Dunstan (the patron saint of ringers) with others set up a school at Tours for training missionaries.

There have been many changes to the building over the centuries. The nave was rebuilt in the thirteenth century with an aisle on either side. In 1757 the spire was built onto the Norman tower. An entire new ring of bells were cast in 1781, increasing from six to eight with a further two added in 1787. As well as being used for normal church services, the bells have pealed for less familiar occasions. The Pancake Bell was rung at Shrove-tide to call people to confession and to warn the women to use up all the lard and dripping before the abstinence of meat. This was then used to make pancakes. The Sanctus Bell rang three times at the blessing of the bread then a further three after the blessing of the wine during the office of the mass. The Morning

ST. MARTIN'S CATHEDRAL, LEICESTER.

40

Bell would herald folk to start their daily work. In 1862 the north porch was renovated and the spire we have now was added in 1867.

The Church of St Martin was given cathedral status on the reconstitution of the Leicester diocese in 1927. The cathedral is open to the public at varying times and attracts many visitors. It is light and airy, has a welcoming atmosphere, and is certainly not the kind of place one would expect to encounter a ghost.

However, two separate incidents may put this in doubt. In April 1996 a choral concert was performed by the South Wales Ynysowen Choir. After the soprano had finished her piece, a freeman tactfully asked the compère of the event if she had noticed anything unusual during the soprano's performance. The compère replied that she had noticed nothing unusual whatsoever. The puzzled man then told her of a woman with white hair and wearing a long white gown who had come to stand between the compère and the soprano. The compère thought it odd but soon dismissed the matter.

At the end of the concert a friend of the compère who had distributed programmes had been told by a member of the audience that they had seen a strange-looking woman moving around the side aisles during the performance by the soprano. She had white hair and was dressed in a long white gown. A week later another sighting during the event also came to light; the witness this time also mentioned experiencing a strange hot and cold sensation.

On a humorous note, given the fact that Leicester Guildhall is less than a stone's throw away from the cathedral, one may be forgiven for considering the idea that the ghost of Agnes Clarke might have yet again flaunted the idea that ghosts are confined to one area.

The other encounter took place in St George's Chapel. A lady was idly looking at some regimental exhibits when she saw someone whom she assumed was the verger slowly entering the chapel through a door. The lady was then shocked to see the man she assumed to be the verger simply vanish into thin air. As if this was not odd enough, the door from which the figure had entered vanished with him!

Opposite: *The cathedral, scene of some rather odd happenings.*

Right: *St George's Chapel, a figure seemingly entered through a non-existent door.*

Above left: *The building where the typists were spooked by an unseen but noisy presence.*

Above right: *St Mary's Church; just who or what followed the lad?*

Friar Lane

This part of Leicester is an area where most of the buildings are occupied by architects, accountants, solicitors and offices for various companies. During the day the area is very busy, but in the evening when everyone has gone home, the place becomes quite deserted.

There used to be stories of a ghost inhabiting one of the buildings that originates from the early 1800s. Nothing was ever seen but noises of someone storming about the place were reported on several occasions.

In the 1920s the building was converted into offices. Everything seemed quite normal until one night when two young typists stayed late in order to catch up with some urgent paperwork.

Suddenly, above the clatter of the two typewriters, they heard heavy footsteps emanating from the floor above. They stopped typing and listened. They knew they were alone in the building, so who or what was it? The footsteps were then heard to move towards the staircase then begin to descend. The two girls grabbed their handbags and coats and then with much haste got out of the place.

The next day it was discovered that there had been at least two other such incidents. One involved the addition of slamming doors, which was even worse. As far as I can ascertain there have been no recent disturbances. The ghost is assumed to be that of a fellow who committed suicide in a room on the second floor after his business collapsed.

Another story on Friar Lane, which occurred over a short period during the1800s, concerns a young lad being followed some of his way home. The lad would regularly walk home along Friar Lane, over Southgate Street then past the Church of St Mary de Castro. One night as he was halfway along Friar Lane he became aware of footsteps behind him. He looked around and was surprised to see nobody there. He carried on nevertheless. After reaching the church the mysterious footsteps faded out.

This happened on several subsequent occasions. Only once did he actually see anything. On this night at the usual place the footsteps began. The lad hurried his pace, as had become normal practice. He then noticed a shadow moving almost beside him. The shadow appeared to be that of a hunchback with no head. The thing stayed with the lad until the church. The lad turned around to see a grotesque black shadow vanish straight into the closed porch doors.

Greyfriars

A building near Greyfriars was the focus of some very odd goings on between 1995 and 1996. A company dealing in advertising and marketing had occupied the building for only a short period when it became apparent that things were not quite as they should be. One or two employees were convinced of a ghost in the building.

Eventually one of the directors, Mr Harris, thought to approach the local media with the hope of some light being shed on the matter. A reporter from the *Leicester Herald & Post* visited in November 1995. Additionally, a noted clairvoyant was invited along for good measure.

After a tour of every room, corridor and the staircase, the clairvoyant then related the information that had been 'given'. The ghost was a large man with a heart complaint, the man had a passion for cigars (unexplained cigar smoke had been reported), he was in visitation rather than haunting the place and that he had great difficulty climbing the stairs.

The staff dubbed the ghost 'Oscar'. He was not unpleasant in any way, having as much right to be there as anyone. There was one incident involving a filing cabinet that was seen to sway from side to side, which was a little disconcerting of course, plus one young lady claimed to have had her behind pinched by unseen fingers, but on the whole Oscar seemed a gentle chap.

The article in the *Herald & Post* did generate some response. Previous occupants had also reported minor anomalies such as cold spots, a faint presence and the smell of cigar smoke in an oak-panelled room on the ground floor. It was also established that the building had previously been a school and a hospital. Originally the building was a gentleman's residence and the man who built it tragically died on the very day he should have moved in.

The Guildhall

The Leicester Guildhall was built around 1390 by the Gild of Corpus Christi, a lay religious body. The gild carried much weight, giving precedence over the Mayor and the council.

Following the dissolution of the monasteries in the 1530s, the Gild of Corpus Christi was dissolved. The Guildhall was then later acquired by a Mrs Cecelia Pickerell and in 1563 the

The Guildhall, a place with much history.

Leicestershire Corporation purchased the building for the princely sum of £25 15s 4d. In 1588 the Guildhall hosted a banquet in order to celebrate the defeat of the Spanish Armada. Many dignitaries attended the prestigious feast, including Walter Hastings who commanded the troops for the defence against the Armada.

On 16 September 1642, Prince Rupert, Commander of the Royal Forces, demanded £2,000 from the Mayor and the corporation. Charles I, Prince Rupert's uncle, was then approached regarding the matter by the town's Mayor as the corporation could only secure a bounty of £500. The King, after consideration, then wavered the remainder of the money. Further troubles ensued three years later when the Siege of Leicester commenced. The King attacked Leicester to divert the Parliamentarians from attacking Oxford. The Royalists outnumbered the Leicester defences by three to one. After a brave and bloody defeat the Leicester troops surrendered. The Royalists then pillaged the Guildhall, removing the Great Mace among many other valuable items.

The Guildhall has played host to a vast variety of functions over the centuries. Much of Shakespeare's work was acted out in the Great Hall and legend has it that the Bard himself once put in an appearance. Book sales, lectures, entertainers all used the Guildhall and one somewhat bizarre annual event that preceded a huge banquet was the 'Mock Hunt of the Hare.' This involved throwing a dead cat into a tub of aniseed water. The wretched animal was then tied to a horse's tail before being dragged through the streets from Daneshill. A while later a group of huntsmen and a pack of hounds would follow the trail of the 'hare', eventually arriving at the Guildhall for the celebratory dinner. Bear baiting took place on numerous occasions. This barbaric form of 'entertainment' involved a bear being led into the Great Hall where it would be chained to a specially constructed post. A number of mastiffs would be introduced then let loose to attack the poor animal. Thankfully tastes in entertainment have reached a far more civilised nature today and the Great Hall is the setting for a host of activities.

The Guildhall is open to the public as part of Leicester Museums. One may first visit the cells on the ground floor, adjacent to St Martin's West. The Borough Police Force was founded in 1836. The uniform consisted of a blue tailcoat and top hat. They had a rattle to alert colleagues, a wooden truncheon and, on some occasions, they would carry a cutlass. They were housed here in the upper reaches of the building. The cells were a busy place, with all sorts of miscreants crammed in, sometimes as many as nine at a time.

Drunkenness was rife until 1872 when an act was passed whereby alehouses and hotels would close their bars at 11.00 p.m. This made a slight improvement but many a drunken wretch would be thrown into one of the holding cells to sober up.

A good few children have been scared witless over the years while viewing the 'occupants' of the cells. The child would be held up to peer into total darkness through the small viewing hatch. The fiendish parent would then push a brass button next to the hatch. This would activate a light to reveal a scruffily dressed and very dusty wax dummy sitting on the wooden bench opposite the hatch, producing total terror, fleetingly though, as the child would invariably demand, 'Can I have another look?' I am pleased to report that this tradition carries on to this day.

This part of the building does seem rather eerie. Some have commented on the chilliness and gloomy atmosphere. An 'iron maiden' hanging impassively does little to lighten the mood. Like a rusting skeleton, the thing is a grim reminder of harsh punishment and sufferance. Perhaps this sufferance is somehow held in time to be 'replayed' periodically, causing certain individuals of a sensitive nature to feel stifled, or for 'goose pimples' to rise and hair to lift. An apparition apparently has been observed here: a large man, with a full beard, his general appearance 'tatty' and he shambled about as if confused. During the manifestation a tangible feeling of hopelessness

Above: *The Guildhall's quiet little courtyard.*

Opposite: *A cell with 'inmate' who bears a passing resemblance to a mysterious figure glimpsed nearby.*

and depression seemed to emanate from the silent figure. A strong smell of leather hung in the air after the manifestation disappeared.

Out in the little courtyard there is supposed to be a large, black phantom hound that lopes about in an agitated manner. This apparition has only been reported on one occasion. A sound of someone wearing stout boots was once heard crossing the courtyard, but there was no one to be seen.

Several years ago much structural work was undertaken and an extension to the visitor's centre and a cafeteria was added. The site for this project was to be on a small, private graveyard at the rear of the property. Over a hundred bodies were exhumed. I recall visiting the Guildhall shortly into the improvement work and chatting to museum assistant Tony Webster, a great character and a walking history book. I watched a small group of workmen carefully exhuming remains and said jokingly to Tony, 'Well, if this doesn't stir the ghosts up, nothing will.' And, apparently it did. There have been several instances in the cafeteria where chairs moved of their own volition and an unseen hand rings the service bell on the counter.

A small staircase in the courtyard leads up to the library. These rooms are thought to have originally been the living quarters of the chantry priest of the Corpus Christi Gild. In 1632 the Town Library was moved here from St Martin's Church. It is the third oldest public library in England. The library houses many rare and ancient volumes. Books may be viewed by prior arrangement.

The stairs leading up to the Guildhall library. Perhaps it was the phantom black cat that caused Mary to fall to her death?

This area is the haunting ground of the White Lady. She is thought to be a lady called Mary, who fell headlong down the stairs and died as a result. She was buried in the little private graveyard. Much of the time this ghost chooses to remain anonymous and is rarely seen. She is assumed though, to be responsible for nocturnal interference with a large King James I Bible. The bible rests on a long banqueting table and is often left on a particular passage by inquisitive staff at closing time. Not always are the cunning staff successful with the 'trap' they have set, but occasionally on arriving in the morning the bible's pages ore on a totally different passage.

Norman Gambin, who has been with the museum service for over thirty years, has only had one notable experience that may be attributed to the White Lady. One late afternoon, around 5.00 p.m. he had locked the main door on Guildhall Lane. On his return along the passage he heard dainty footsteps from directly above. Norman knew there was no one upstairs, as he was the last to leave. Norman calculated that the footsteps were from the Recorder's Bedroom and part of the library.

The White Lady has only demonstrated her displeasure on one occasion. Early one morning a senior member of the Guildhall staff was contacted by the security company who had overall responsibility for the site, requesting him to urgently proceed to the Guildhall as a burglar alarm had been activated. As a key-holder he duly attended the call-out.

He arrived, entered and went over to the office to view the alarm panel. The readout informed him that an intruder had entered the library. He went upstairs to investigate. He found no sign of a break-in, no broken windows or any other indication of an intruder. He did discover, however, that the banqueting table was some thirty degrees off its usual position. Two stout chairs normally at each end of the table were now positioned at different corners of the room. It was these actions that had activated the movement sensor on the infra-red security unit. There was a minor incident on similar lines during a summer afternoon. The courtyard is a suntrap and Tony was enjoying the sun when an internal alarm went off. Tony found a door leading off from the library that is usually locked had mysteriously opened.

Leaving the library and passing the Recorder's Bedroom, one descends another staircase into the Great Hall. Caution is required here, as a phantom black cat is known to race down the stairs and almost trip people over. The mysterious feline was also seen crossing St Martin's churchyard where it vanished into a grassy bank.

The Great Hall may be haunted, although nothing has actually been seen. Tony Webster opened up at around 7.30 a.m. one December morning in the early 1990s. He had to stoke the fire up in the Great Hall as it was quite cold. He suddenly heard loud footsteps from the roof space that could not be explained.

The Guildhall presently lays claim to be 'Leicester's most haunted building' and presents popular ghost story evenings. Usually around Halloween and Christmas an audience will sit in the Great Hall where Blue Badge tour guides will relate spine-chilling ghost stories. Most recently a new event has been introduced which is highly popular: 'Ghostwatch'. This allows members of the public the opportunity to spend the dark hours in small groups of observation teams hunting out the ghosts, an ideal experience for the ghost enthusiast.

Guildhall Lane

Guildhall lane is a quiet little thoroughfare from Applegate to Loseby Lane. It used to be called Townhall Lane. It comprises a shop, two restaurants, a Victorian factory still with a cobbled

David Vaughan; is this the silent figure that strolls the area?

yard, the Guildhall, the cathedral and part of a school. At either side of the cathedral are narrow cobbled alleys, St Martin's East and St Martin's West. At night the place can take on a very lonely feel.

A mysterious phantom known as the Black Friar or the Man in Black is alleged to wander Guildhall Lane and some of the adjacent areas. Apparently, he is thought to have been a devoted clergyman who died suddenly, is unaware of his predicament, and still has unfinished business to attend to. His perambulations are usually late at night but once he was seen in broad daylight. A lady was looking into a jewellery shop window on the corner of Guildhall Lane and Loseby Lane one afternoon when she was struck by a reflected image of a very tall figure with a wide brimmed hat almost behind her. She turned around but the figure had vanished into thin air.

In 1980 a young man walking along Guildhall Lane in the early hours observed a tall man with a long coat or cloak and wearing a clerical hat walking towards him. The tall man then left the pavement to cross over but faded out into nothing.

On Good Friday 1993, a couple who were going to sit on one of the benches in St Martin's churchyard for a while had a strange experience. They walked down St Martin's West to cut through when the man noticed someone standing facing the wall of the Vaughan Porch, a tall man wearing a long, dark garment, though there was no hat in evidence. They both watched and found it odd that the man was so still and unaware that he was being observed. Also, the figure must have heard the couple talking but seemed not to notice. The lady felt intimidated so the couple moved out of view for a few seconds before looking again. The figure was gone. The couple were convinced they had confronted a ghost. Some have speculated that this figure could be the shade of one of the Vaughan family.

The Vaughan's settled in Leicester in 1763. Henry Vaughan bought a house on New Street. His grandson, Edward Thomas, served as a vicar at St Martin's. Three of Edward's sons, Charles John,

Edward Thomas and David James, carried on the tradition, the latter held an incumbency from 1860 until 1893. He was obviously beloved of his church, turning down a living in Battersea at £1,200 a year while his living at St Martin's was a comparatively modest £140 per annum. He was also renowned for his efforts with improving vaccinations and adult education. He founded the Leicester Working Men's College that later evolved to the Vaughan College on St Nicholas Circle. Why would not a man perhaps appear sometimes to reflect?

A woman police constable noticed a similarly clad figure strolling along Guildhall Lane late one evening. The WPC assumed the man was on his way home from a fancy dress party. She followed him past the Guildhall, then onto St Martin's West. At almost halfway along, the figure promptly vanished.

On the night of Easter Sunday 2001 a guided ghost walk was in progress. At around 9.30 p.m., the guide and small group were positioned on St Martin's West. The guide was halfway through relating the story of the sighting on Good Friday 1993 when a figure almost identical to that he was describing passed the top of the alley by the Guildhall. Only he saw it as everyone else was facing him. The stunned guide thought not to mention this as it might have appeared as 'staged'.

Interestingly these accounts differ in that a hat is present on only two of the alleged sightings. Are we to believe there might be two very similar entities in this area?

The Opera House

On the corner of Guildhall Lane and St Martin's East stands a building most local people will remember as a sewing machine manufacturer, the premises of Walter O'Brien Ltd. The building is now an award-winning restaurant, the Opera House.

The property was originally part of St George's Hall and was used by the Guild of St George before the Reformation. This was demolished around 1680.

It is believed that an inn stood on the site in 1460. According to the deeds, the building was later converted to two messuages (dwelling houses with outbuildings and land assigned to it) with 20 acres near to Abbey Gate.

From 1706 until 1770 a family called the Needhams resided there. Shortly after, one of the messuages, No. 10 Townhall Lane, became an alehouse, the Queen's Head Inn. At the weekends the overflow of drunks who could not be found accommodation in the Guildhall cells would be locked in parts of the large cellars of the inn; this is ironic as some proportion of the drunkards must have been in here in the first place!

In September 1896 both properties, Nos 10 and 12 were converted to the Opera House Hotel. This alehouse slowly gained a reputation as a 'rough house' and a brothel. As a result the place was closed down in 1914.

For five years an antique shop occupied the site then Walter O'Brien took it over in 1920. His business remained until 1998 when Noel and Val Weafer purchased the Grade II-listed building.

Two years of red tape (with it being listed) and extensive renovation was carried out with much of the original features preserved. The restaurant opened its doors in 2000.

The first indication that something was not quite right came in the form of a presence. Nothing nasty but nevertheless it was odd. This tended to be sensed usually after a busy night and often on a Saturday.

Left: *The Opera House, an award-winning restaurant.*

Below: The *Church Room, originally a small cottage.*

Over a long period the presence slowly seemed to become more prominent in a part of the restaurant called the Church Room. Some of the staff told Val they felt uncomfortable around the area at times and a few left due to the feeling of unrest. There were several instances where knives would fall off a particular table for no apparent reason.

Val admits to noticing an atmosphere change near the Church Room, which is where one of the messuages would have stood, No. 12.

Later on there were comments from waitresses of 'something' in the lower floor of the restaurant, the old cellars. On one occasion, after closing, a figure was seen moving in the cellar on the CCTV unit. On investigation there was no one down there. There was also a sighting of a dark figure sitting near one of the tables reported by one waitress who was clearing up.

The oddest event occurred towards the end of a busy Saturday evening in 2002. A couple were in the small lobby and bar area settling their bill. Val was sorting out the credit card machine. When Val looked up she noticed the lady looking a little pale and edgy. Only seconds before the lady had moved aside as she caught sight of a man wearing a white shirt. The man then walked through the wall. Only she saw it. Val was most sympathetic about the matter and made light of it.

There is an unsubstantiated story that when the site was occupied by the Opera House Hotel a 'client' refused to pay for the services of one of the prostitutes. A violent scuffle then resulted in the drunken man being stabbed to death – could this explain the alleged ghost?

Val believes there may be more than one ghost. She was informed that there had been a woman seen near the doorway of the restaurant who faded out into nothing when approached. Val learned that there used to be a Mrs Kale who lived for many years in one of the little messuages. She was apparently very attached to the place and happy there. For the moment, Val remains tolerant of the ghost(s) as there have been no major problems, so far.

St Martin's Churchyard

One of Leicester's most well known phantoms is the mysterious hooded figure that is said to crouch under or near a tree in the churchyard. Some think it may be a leper or plague victim while others have assumed it to be a monk from the long gone Greyfriars Monastery. I was told that a ghostly monk emerges from St Martin's East then crosses the graveyard before slowly vanishing near the Leicester Grammar School playground.

There have been no recent sightings reported. This might be due to the churchyard being drastically altered in 1987. This was in order to widen the drive up to the main porch. Many of the gravestones are now formed in a semi-circle behind a path leading to a small fountain.

On a hot, humid night in 1976 a young couple were sitting on one of the benches engaged in idle chat. It was just after dusk, around 8.30 p.m. After a while the girl seemed transfixed by a weird mist under a tree. 'It's just a cloud of gnats,' offered the young man. The girl was adamant that it was not gnats. The young man got up and walked over. As he approached, the 'mist' dissipated as a cloud of gnats would. 'See, it's just gnats.' She responded, 'It's still there, it isn't gnats.' Eventually whatever it was faded and the couple went on their way. The girl was convinced of 'something going on'.

There is an old legend attached to this misty phantom. Those who are unlucky enough to see it would be prudent to give it a wide berth. Should it reach out and drag its icy fingers across your face you will be dead within the year.

St Martin's East, a phantom monk commences his short perambulations here.

St Martin's churchyard: the spot where the Victorian couple were seen to form then glide along.

There have been several sighting of a lady and a man dressed in Victorian clothes in the churchyard. The couple simply 'emerge' as if from nowhere then casually stroll through the churchyard, then glide out onto St Martin's where they dissipate. One curious witness later investigated and it emerged there was a couple interred here around the late eighteenth century in the proximity of where the couple were seen to form.

In recent times, the churchyard has become a popular place for 'goths' to hang out. For the uninformed, goths are mainly young individuals with a passion for the lugubrious side of life. They tend to favour black and purple clothes with cadaverous make-up. So, be warned, if passing through the churchyard at night, the goths may look more ghostly than the ghosts!

St Nicholas' Church

St Nicholas Circle is a busy route for much of the traffic entering the city. It is fairly nondescript and comprises a few shops, a large hotel, a multistorey car park and a museum that is situated by Jewry Wall. This structure is the second largest remaining example of Roman masonry in England. Jewry Wall was constructed around AD 130, it is 24ft high, 75ft long and 8ft thick. The wall is built of Derbyshire stone and Leicestershire granite. The adjacent museum, which occupies the site, allows one to meander around the old Roman baths in front of the wall. There have, apparently, been occasional glimpses of figures dressed in Roman togas moving about the ruins.

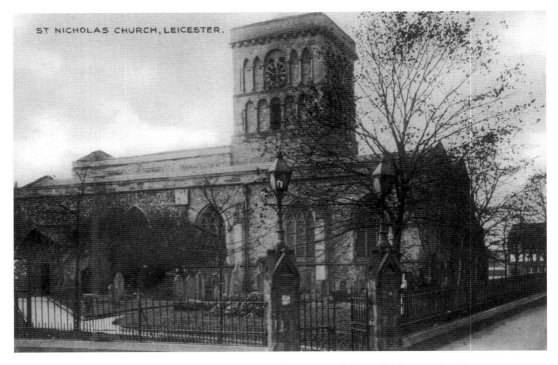

Above: *St Nicholas's Church, an ancient site.*

Left: *The narrow doorway where the dark figure stood.*

On the other side of Jewry Wall stands the Church of St Nicholas. This Anglo-Saxon church was built around AD 880. Much Roman brickwork is incorporated into the structure. In the churchyard near the main porch there is part of a Roman pillar still in evidence. Several changes to the building have been undertaken, the most drastic being the removal of the spire in 1803.

A narrow alley between the wall and the church, St Nicholas Walk, takes one through to the quaintly named Holy Bones. Just to the right, a small gateway allows access to the rear of the churchyard.

It was here that Barry Spencer (then aged ten) had a strange experience in early November. 1957. Barry had come to await his father who worked at a factory almost opposite the rear of the churchyard. The time was just before 5.00 p.m. From here they would visit the slipper baths at Vestry Street. There were one or two people leaving for home. The fashion for men at this time was mainly stout, long overcoats and either a flat cap or a trilby-type hat. The figure Barry was observing did not seem to fit in somehow. The man was standing stock still almost in the narrow gateway. He wore a long black coat or cloak and a stiff, black, wide-brimmed hat. Although the figure was illuminated by gas lamp, his face was in shadow. After a minute or two, Barry felt intimidated and moved away. When his father arrived shortly after, Barry told him about the strange man, who by now had gone.

Barry can remember the experience 'as if it was yesterday'. While describing the figure he likened it to the symbol used for advertising 'Sandeman's Port', a mysterious figure in black. 'I don't really believe in ghosts as such, but there was definitely something odd about that character, he just didn't make sense,' Barry concluded.

Wygston's House

On the leafy little Applegate opposite Leicester Grammar School stands Wygston's House or, as it was known locally, the Costume Museum. It is believed that the wealthy wool merchant Roger Wygston lived here in the fifteenth century. There is some debate here, as the assumption is based on the letters R.W. painted onto one of the windows. Another successful wool merchant, William Rowlatt, might have lived here. Presumably if it were the latter the initials would be in reverse order.

In any case, it is a very grand place indeed. Many will remember the creaking floorboards and the mannequins dressed in costumes reflecting the fashion throughout the centuries. Upstairs one could sit and flip through fashion magazines, or merely admire the splendid timber workings of the upper parts. At times the house was restful, sometimes eerily quiet.

At the rear there were two mock-up shops, a clothing purveyor's and a general grocer's. It was interesting to view an insight into the retail customs of the early nineteenth century.

The museum was a popular place for parties of schoolchildren. Heaps of costumes, fancy dress articles, hats and all manner of adornments would be provided. With much gusto, the children would dress up and have a most enjoyable (if somewhat noisy) time. On some occasions, another child would join in.

Jonathon, as some have referred to him, is a boy of around ten years old. He dresses in clothes of the Georgian period, and, like all boys, he is prone to a bit of mischief. Several visiting children have played 'hide and seek' with him, blissfully unaware that Jonathon always wins. He appears and disappears at will. He is not always seen but certainly makes his presence known if he is having a temper tantrum. Museum assistant, Tony Webster told of an incident where his wife

Wygston's House, home to little Jonathon.

was upstairs chatting to some visitors, when suddenly a large chair swung violently around in a complete circle on the polished floor as if pushed by unseen hands.

Another member of staff opened up early one morning and distinctly heard the sound of a child sobbing somewhere in the proximity. After going back outside for a second or two in case the crying was someone nearby, the assistant re-entered and was stunned to glimpse the boy at the foot of the stairs crying.

As to who Jonathon is, remains unclear. Whether his name came about as a nickname or was projected psychically is uncertain. Perhaps the sobbing was an indication Jonathon somehow knew of the eventual closure of the museum. The building was empty for some time but is presently in use. Anyone who might encounter Jonathon should perhaps show not fear, but compassion, as he is more than likely missing his little playmates.

TWO

BRAUNSTONE HALL

The History

The first records of Braunstone are found in Domesday Book of 1086. It is referred to as Brantestone.

After the Norman Conquest much of England was divided amongst William the Conquerer's noblemen. Hugh de Grantesmesnil took Braunstone; he was one of William I's most powerful barons and was given many manors in Leicestershire and further afield. In 1246 Roger de Queney owned the land. After his death it passed on to the Ferres of Groby. Between the thirteenth and sixteenth centuries, the Harecourts owned the estate. In the late sixteenth century some of the land was sold off. The Manners family of Aylestone bought 150 acres. The Bennet family then purchased 100 acres of land. By 1607, 468 acres of land had become pasture.

The Winstanley family came to Leicester in the 1750s. James Winstanley, a successful solicitor, bought the estate for £6,000. The family resided in an Elizabethan manor near to Braunstone Lane.

In 1775 Clement Winstanley commissioned William Oldham, an architect and builder, to design and build Braunstone Hall, a red brick, five-bays-wide, two-and-a-half storey Georgian mansion house.

In the mid-1800s, James Beaumont Winstanley inherited the estate, then mysteriously disappeared while on a trip to Europe in 1862. His sister Anne Jane Pochin later inherited the estate which she passed down to her son Richard Norman Pochin in 1904. He changed his name by deed poll to Winstanley. He had modernisation work carried out on the building in 1911, adding an extension to the north-east side of the property and introducing a gas engine, which would be used for operating an early form of central heating.

A compulsory purchase order was placed on the land in 1924. The park was opened to the public in the early 1930s. The hall was later adapted to serve as a junior school.

During the Second World War, both the hall and the park housed detachments of the Home Guard, the Royal Artillery and the American 82nd Airborne Division.

Today the park is a typical oasis with two lakes and a stream, woodland and spinneys with plenty of free space for kite enthusiasts, joggers, dog walkers and is of course ideal for those wishing to partake in football, cricket and other sporting activities. At the time of writing, the hall is empty.

The Haunting

Over the years, the area has gained a reputation for being haunted. Some of the young Winstanley's and even the servants were less than enthusiastic to have to wander some of the

The enigmatic Braunstone Hall around the early 1900s.

dark corridors of the hall with just a candle for company. One evening in 1922, Rosemary Winstanley was walking along the top floor corridor when she confronted a figure dressed in white or cream robes. The figure moved swiftly over and entered the governess's room. It was later discovered that two of Rosemary's aunties, May and Georgina, had left the hall to become nuns in a Roman Catholic convent. Why they should have both wished to leave their comfortable surroundings for such an austere life is unclear. May tragically died in Southampton after succumbing to consumption in 1899, aged only eighteen. This disease was especially prevalent among young adults and was incurable at the time. The governess's room used to be occupied by May Winstanley. It has been suggested that the ghost is that of May as she was a novice nun, who wore white robes.

There have been several reports of a dark and silent horse-drawn carriage, assumed to be a hearse as the horses are black, that passes the hall then in the dead of night vanishes near the old spinney.

During the period the school was housed at the hall there were claims of poltergeist-type phenomena such as pencils flipping up in the air, girls having their pigtails pulled, workmen's tools being hidden or moved overnight and strange lights up at the windows flashing on and off. As a result of the strange lights the police were dispatched on several occasions. One evening the key-holder was called out. When he arrived there was a police dog and handler as well as another officer. They all entered the hall. The German Shepherd seemed interested in the main staircase. It began to ascend then stopped. It was looking intently up the stairs as if reacting to

The corridor and room where the ghost of May Winstanley is said to walk.

someone. The officers saw nothing at all. Eventually the key-holder and police officers finished their investigation. The building was found to be empty and locked as on all previous occasions. One key-holder spoke of a memorable occasion where he and police arrived as a call had been received that lights were on in a top-floor room at nearly midnight. The lights could be seen from a distance but as the party approached the lights dimmed out. To add to the mystery this occurred during a period when improvement works were underway and so the electricity supply had been isolated.

A caretaker at the school encountered a petite, white-robed figure on numerous occasions. The figure would usually appear on the top-floor corridor, most often on a winter's dusk when all the children and most of the staff had left. The caretaker apparently became quite used to seeing the figure and made no fuss about it.

In 1988 a charity ghost event was staged. Persons were sponsored to spend the night in the building. Nothing unusual was seen or heard but a local radio reporter recorded footsteps that were not heard at the time of making the tape.

A Night of Clairvoyance

In 1989 renowned local historian, Brian Johnson, who was also vice-chairman of the Leicester Fellowship for Psychic Studies, set about arranging a night in the school to find out if there was any substance in the idea of the place being haunted. He paid a preliminary visit to meet the headmaster then have a tour of the school. A date was arranged for the proposed all-night study then the school secretary, Shirley Richards, showed Brian around this deceptively large building.

On entering one small room, Brian felt a change in temperature. As he was about to comment on this to Shirley he saw out of the corner of his eye a small child wearing a red garment over by a window. As he turned to look properly the vision disappeared. Shirley had expressed much interest in the idea of the hall being haunted and was perplexed at not seeing anything herself. She was keen to volunteer to stay up with the small group on the coming night. It would make a change to be in there while it was quiet, as during the day the place was full of noisy children.

The night came and with much enthusiasm the small group planned their strategy. Brian had brought along a video camera to record the event. Shirley's sister, Lynn, was there as well as she was also fascinated. Two 'guest' psychics from outside of Leicestershire completed the party.

Very early on into the evening, the first apparition was sensed then seen to form: an elderly lady sitting in the main hall. The psychic received impressions that the lady was very attached to the place and had a love of music. At around midnight, three apparitions formed on the stairs, a man and two ladies, one of the guest psychics claimed. The trio were dressed grandly and were either returning from or were on their way to a ball. Brian saw nothing but filmed anyway. It was quickly noted that these were interactive rather than just wandering spirits. Shirley was disappointed at the subjective information from the psychics and frustrated at not seeing anything herself. The ghosts, particularly a lady in a rich ballgown, were very bemused by the attention, the psychic claimed. The lady seemed interested in Lynn and several witnesses (including Shirley) observed Lynn's clothes 'ripple' as if being plucked at.

Brian went on several meanders of the building, sometimes with company and on one such tour a definite smell of flowers was noted in the vicinity of May Winstanley's old room. On his solo patrols, Brian felt unsettled a couple of times but saw or heard nothing unusual.

Towards the end of their study period at 4.00 a.m., a final encounter was experienced by just one member of the group. On descending the staircase, one lady turned to her son who had stopped still and saw the look of shock on his face. She asked what was up. Apparently he casually glanced back at the passage and saw a mist swiftly move across the corridor towards the room of May Winstanley. Brian quickly ran over and checked the room, but there was nothing there.

After the group had departed Shirley and Lynn went up to the staffroom on the first floor. They had arranged to stay on until the caretaker arrived and had prepared makeshift sleeping arrangements in the form of camp beds and a few blankets. Their much-needed rest was soon to be disturbed however. A series of distant bangs echoing through the building brought them both fully awake. Shirley interpreted the sounds to be as if someone was storming about the hall banging the doors. Neither Shirley nor Lynn felt compelled to investigate. After a short period the sounds ceased.

The Exterior

Ghostly goings on, it seems, are not confined to the interior of the building. As well as the horse-drawn carriage, it is alleged there is an active area in the proximity of a 70ft-high cedar tree at the rear of the hall. It is believed that a child once fell from it and was mortally wounded. Also there is alleged to have been two incidents of persons hanging themselves from a horizontal branch some 8ft from the ground. Nothing is seen but occasionally a feeling of dread and uneasiness is

A young groom met an untimely death in the old stables at Braunstone Hall.

remarked upon. One young man was surprised to hear a loud thud near the tree as if a heavy weight had been dropped. He looked around but found no explanation whatsoever.

The glades and spinney to the south-west can be a little daunting. A ghostly child, a girl of around twelve years old, is said to wander here. One visitor was convinced that she was being followed but could see no one around. There is also a rumour of some kind of malevolent presence around the old stables. Apparently a young groom was found hanging from a timber beam in a room above the stables.

There is a mystery involving a man cycling through Braunstone Park on a Sunday morning in 1988. He was unfamiliar with the park but thought to cycle through it as it was a pleasant day and he was in no hurry. He noticed two horses in a fenced paddock to the right of the hall facing Hinckley Road. He was mildly surprised, as the park has something of a reputation for groups of youths causing trouble and the horses seemed quite vulnerable.

It would be seventeen years later when the man would hear a segment of a radio programme featuring Braunstone Park. During the broadcast it was mentioned that up until the early 1920s there used to be two horses kept in a paddock. Intrigued, the man has tried to get to the bottom of this affair. At the time of writing it has been established that there were no horses or a fenced -off field around the time the man claimed. The matter remains unsatisfactorily resolved.

The Medium and the Historian

In April 1994, a well-known medium visited the Braunstone Hall. The evening event was for a short television programme and magazine feature. The format involved the medium touring the building, then having a historian brought in afterwards to comment on any information that was received psychically.

Top Hat Terrace: master of disguise Tanky Smith's former palatial residence.

After the two-hour experiment the medium was introduced to historian John Bayldon, an authority on Braunstone Hall. The medium then related her information. She was initially struck by the sheer volume of spirit energy within the building. It was as if most of those who lived here were unwilling to move on. In a second-floor classroom was a young girl in a long white garment; she was sitting down and engaged in writing a letter. She was suffering from an incurable chest illness and was a novice nun. She had no fear of death and a feeling of tranquillity filled the room. In another classroom, the atmosphere was that of dread. The medium picked up on two apparitions, a gentleman and a young girl, a serving wench, who appeared to be around fifteen years old. The man was telling the tearful wench that gentlemen did not marry servant girls. Later on, downstairs, the medium confronted a large man. He suffered from gout. The last impression of the evening was, most oddly, a pig that was glimpsed trotting hastily along a corridor.

John Bayldon could offer no record of any incidents involving a man or a servant girl. Also the man with gout did not register in any way, although a stonemason and a labourer were both killed when scaffolding collapsed during the building of the house. Perhaps the supposed apparition reflected one of these tragedies. John commented that the figure in white would be, without doubt, May Winstanley as there had been so many descriptive sightings. The matter of the pig impressed John Bayldon greatly, and with much humour he explained that at one time there was a menagerie and it was known that a pig had bitten a visitor. What became of it is uncertain though.

John then related the mystery of the 'vanishing Winstanley'. As mentioned earlier, John Beaumont Winstanley went missing whilst travelling in Europe in 1862. The family enlisted the help of Francis (Tanky) Smith, Britain's first private detective, to track him down. His arduous task eventually led him to Coblentz in Germany where a badly decomposed body had been washed up on the bank of the River Moselle. One of the servants was sent over and identified a remaining cufflink. It was then established that the remains were that of James Beaumont Winstanley.

On his return, Francis Smith was paid very handsomely indeed, reportedly 1,000 guineas. He used the proceeds to put towards building a house on London Road. As a folly he had several busts carved of him in his many disguises and placed along the upper fascia. Top Hat Terrace is still there for all to see. Its stone depictions of Smith in his many disguises are quite intact and perfectly preserved.

John mused that he thought there was something sinister about the matter. He felt adamant that James Beaumont Winstanley was murdered at the hall. He expressed a desire to see what the lifting of heavy flagstones in the cellar might uncover.

The Ghost Researchers

Later in the 1994 a small party of ghost researchers examined the case in order to see if there was evidence of any ghostly activity at the hall. Ideally, this meant hard evidence rather than subjective impressions or anecdotal accounts.

Additionally, scientific apparatus would be applied during some of the study periods. This evaluation included a night spent in the building. Video cameras, tripod-mounted still cameras and tape recorders were set up. Two rooms were chosen as 'controlled areas'. This entailed securing the room with random articles placed and marked within. Any entrance to the room was then 'sealed' by a network of threads that were then secured with a signed seal. The idea for this experiment is simple. If at the end of the study period the random articles placed are disturbed and the seals are intact, this may indicate 'genuine' ghostly activity.

The night passed fairly quietly, although there was one incident that caused a bit of excitement. While all but two of the team were in the staffroom having a short coffee break, a faint but audible scream was heard; it seemed to emanate from the staircase. Steve and Ian, who were up on the second-floor landing heard this, then they both 'felt something' move behind them very rapidly. Simultaneously, a small device Ian was holding that reacted to surges in electrical voltage began to feel very hot then momentarily glowed. Ian had never known this to happen before.

If nothing else, the ghost researchers provided Shirley with a long-awaited dream. After one uneventful evening visit, the ghost researchers were on the forecourt chatting. Suddenly an excited Shirley came over and exclaimed, 'I've seen it'. Apparently, as Shirley was waiting for the caretaker, Jeff, to set the alarm, which was acting up for some reason, she casually glanced up the old servant's staircase. She was astonished to see an incandescent misty shape that 'moved back' out of sight, as if not wanting to be seen.

The summary of the ghost researchers indicated that there might have been some form of discarnate entity attached to the building. The experiments failed to bring anything new to the case however, but there was certainly no question of deception.

In August 1996 Braunstone Hall Junior School closed.

The Friends

After the closure of the school, the building became the target of repeated vandalism. Steel shutters were fixed to the lower windows, a large security light was fitted and the upper windows

Braunstone Hall today, hopefully a new lease of life will be enjoyed by this special place.

were reinforced with polycarbonate (unbreakable clear plastic) covers. These measures did seem to stem the tide of almost nightly attacks on the place.

A sorry state of affairs indeed; one group of vandals actually managed to get into the building by literally knocking part of a wall out! Then the arson attacks began. Amazingly though, the building has stood defiant of the constant abuse.

In February 2005, the Friends of Braunstone Hall was formed. Founders, Dorian and Kim Gamble decided it was high time to do something about it. Enthusiastic volunteers would periodically patrol the area and clean up the mess outside the hall. Police would be informed if potential trouble might present itself.

Their work has already made a huge difference. One may visit without broken bottles, tin cans and other litter to wade through. It was on one morning cleaning-up operation that Dorian had a strange experience. He was at the front of the hall when a concentrated grey mist passed him at incredible speed. Dorian had heard of the ghosts but had paid little notice, until now.

On the morning of Friday 10 May, John Bayldon came to visit to relate the history of the building. He was astonished at how well the interior looked after nine years of being unused. Halfway through his lecture on the parlour a scream disrupted the proceedings. Dorian's daughter Emma came tearfully into the parlour. As she was descending the old servants' stairs, she observed a shadow on the wall moving upwards. She then experienced a nasty sensation as if 'something' had passed right through her.

It is hoped the building will shortly get a new lease of life. Various plans are in early stages with residents groups and other bodies. On an open day in August 2005, Rosemary Winstanley returned. The frail but enthusiastic lady spoke of her sighting of the nun in 1922 and said she would return here in spirit like so many have before.

THREE

CASTLE PARK

Bow Bridge

'Look at him, the monk,' exclaimed the amazed barmaid to her husband who had picked her up from the pub on King Richard's Road. Her husband saw nothing at all. They both looked back but the monk had gone. Why would a phantom monk be standing on Bow Bridge anyway?

Bow Bridge is on the busy A47, coming into Leicester from the west. The original Roman stone bridge was demolished in 1862. The bridge of today was constructed in 1883. It is of iron and is decorated with the white and red roses of the Dukes of Lancaster and York.

Richard III was born in October 1452. He was a regular visitor to Leicester and would often stay at Leicester Castle.

After King Edward IV died in 1483, his eldest son, Edward (Richard's nephew) should have inherited the throne. It was, however, found that Edward and his brother were illegitimate. Richard was crowned King on 6 July of that year.

Prior to becoming King, Richard had strong support in the north. His reliance on the northerners increased during his reign, causing resentment in the south. On 7 August 1485 Henry Tudor arrived in Wales with an army of Lancastrian exiles, intent on claiming the throne.

Orders were sent out for his northern supporters to join him at Nottingham. Those from the south would meet him in Leicester.

On the dawn of 22 August, Richard rode out of Leicester over the old Bow Bridge to the Battle of Bosworth, the last battle of the Wars of the Roses. According to an ancient legend, his spur hit a stone on the bridge and an old wise prophet looking on predicted that Richard's head would strike the same stone on his return.

The day after his defeat, Richard's dead and naked body was tied across a horse and then brought back to Leicester. It is said that, as the horse crossed over Bow Bridge, Richard's head struck the same stone as foretold. The last Plantagenet had returned.

His body was displayed for two days in the Church of St Mary of the Annunciation. He was then buried in the chapel of the Greyfriars Monastery. Henry VII donated £10 towards a tomb but this was later desecrated at the dissolution of the monasteries. It is said, although this is legend and not historic fact, that the bones of Richard III were dug up and ordered to be thrown off Bow Bridge into the River Soar. To add insult to injury, his stone coffin apparently ended up as a horse drinking trough near the old White Horse Inn on Gallowtree Gate.

Going on the assumption that a ghost may linger perhaps as a result of murder, tragedy or sufferance, there may be also strong feelings of guilt to tie someone to a situation. Should the bones have been thrown off the bridge to the river below, then who, we must ponder, may have been forced to commit such a damning task – a monk perhaps?

Greyfriars Monastery stood south of St Martin's, occupying the area of Peacock Lane, Friar

The old Bow Bridge as it would have looked in the fourteenth century.

All that remains today of Greyfriars Monastery.

Lane, Southgate and of course Greyfriars. After the dissolution some of the material from the priory chapel was used to repair the Church of St Martin's. All that remains of the monastery, a small area of wall, can be found in a car park on New Street. The car park attendant is used to giving impromptu history lessons and is as disgusted as everyone else at the infinite wisdom of having white painted lines for car bay numbers on a centuries-old chunk of local history!

Carey's Close

There was a spate of unusual goings on in the premises of a sock manufacturer situated on Carey's Close that lasted for a few weeks during 1994.

The works manager, who I will call Mr Teal, had heard rumours going around the factory but thought to take no notice, there was a business to run.

However, his scepticism was ruffled a little early one Sunday morning. Mr Teal and the MD had come in over the weekend to get up to date with some urgent paperwork. They were both sitting at one desk in the general office when their attention was diverted by a faint, dragging sound; they looked around then stared in amazement as a metal wastepaper bin traversed slowly across the carpet, then abruptly stopped. The two men got up, examined the bin and stared at the carpet in total bafflement. Eventually they just carried on with the job in hand. Perhaps there was something to these ghost rumours after all.

A few weeks later one of the secretarial staff came in early one morning. She went into her office and was hit by a blast of freezing cold air. She was then further dazed to see a fine dew covering every surface in the room. Later in the day the maintenance man investigated and found no problem with the heating system. It would have needed a dozen kettles boiling all night to have created the level of vapour for the dew everywhere, a complete mystery.

Down on the work floors there had been claims of various odd events for quite some time. Mysterious pipe smoke, cold spots and a 'tingly' sensation felt by one man, and then the ghost put in an appearance.

A knitter on a late shift watched a fellow loitering near the top of a small staircase at the dispatch bay area. At first the knitter thought it was a tramp. He was around sixty years of age, had grey hair poking out from under a flat, cloth cap and wore a creased, collarless shirt, braces and baggy trousers. His overall appearance was shabby. The knitter also noticed the man had a black oilskin bag of the type that used to adorn bicycle handlebars from around the 1940s to the 1960s. The bag would have contained an enamel mug, sandwiches and whatever else a 'grafter' would have needed to sustain him throughout a working day.

The knitter shouted over but the fellow on the stairs took no notice. Then assuming him to be deaf or unable to hear above the noise from the knitting machines, the knitter went over to see who he was and what he wanted. As he got to the stairs, the man vanished in a flash.

The knitter questioned his own sanity for a day or two then was later delighted to discover that Mr Teal had seen a similar-looking figure in about the same place.

An expert in such matters as ghosts and the occult was approached by Mr Teal; a bit of detective work was needed, according to the expert. After visiting the factory and chatting to one or two of the staff, the expert and Mr Teal sat down in an empty office. The expert explained that working purely from conjecture he could only put forward several theories. The attire of the man seemed to suggest him to be of lower working class; he may well have worked in the building and was attached for some reason. The fact that structural work in the factory tied in with the commencement of the disturbances seemed to strengthen the idea that in some situations, major change can 'stir up' unnatural effects. Not only that but the fact that the office that was created from the building work was where the icy blast and dew effect occurred might indicate the ghost 'making his presence felt'. As for the dew itself, someone had offered the idea that the ghost may be 'showing' his demise. There has been many a factory worker the worse for drink found face down in the River Soar. The expert cheerfully concluded that the clues were there, it was merely a matter of making sense of it all.

The company have now moved premises. I wonder why!

Leicester Castle

The first-time visitor to Leicester would be forgiven in assuming that the Leicester Prison on Welford Road is the castle, what with its turrets and portcullis.

In fact Leicester Castle is on Castle View some half a mile away. The building as we know it was the Crown Court for many years up until the early 1990s.

The original Leicester Castle was of timber construction built upon the nearby motte. The later structure was built in 1150. In 1790 the frontage was modernised to how it looks today. Nothing like a castle at all!

There is reputed to be more than one restless soul wandering the dark and empty building, which is presently part of Leicester Museums. It is not open to the public on a regular basis but

Sunset at Leicester Castle, locked and empty, of the living anyway.

by prior arrangement groups may visit and there are regular guided tours.

Visitors claim to have heard a bell ringing from the cellars when it has been deserted and in darkness. One person sensed a presence that seemed malevolent. This was felt near the main staircase. One visitor, Ian Harvey, took several photographs in the larger of the two courtrooms. On one exposure there appears a bluish light and above this there is a strange image that Ian interprets as resembling a head and upper torso with a rope noose around the neck.

Undoubtedly hangings took place here and beheadings too. The old stone on which the axe would fall is still in evidence on the green outside. Some years ago during works by the water board, no fewer than eleven headless skeletons were found during the excavations. In the cellars there is a pit. This is thought to be where those who were hanged would drop. A cistern nearby was said to have been for the flushing away of bodily fluids. There is a tale of an old dungeon that was discovered in 1634; apparently there were several skeletons still shackled to the walls.

On Saturday 30 October 2004, a party of nurses and theatre staff from Glenfield Hospital spent the night in the building. They were sponsored and the proceeds went towards helping raise funds for specialist equipment. They were mostly highly sceptical and thought of the event as a good night out. But to keep a good balance to the proceedings, the two organisers approached matters with a serious and scientific attitude.

Unfortunately no ghosts were seen but constant malfunction of video cameras seemed to hamper things, which some thought very odd. One of the participants, Mike, commented on his video camera battery pack getting very hot and mysteriously draining of power.

Some say the shade of John of Gaunt haunts the cellars. The fourth son of King Edward III, John of Gaunt was born at Ghent, Flanders in 1340. A man with immense power, among other offices he was guardian to the young Richard II, his nephew, carried the Sword of State in virtue of his Dukedom of Lancaster and he was the carver to the King at the Coronation feast. Of all of John of Gaunt's favourite country abodes, which included Monmouth, Hertford and Lincoln, the castles of Leicester and Kenilworth were his favourites. He died in London on 3 February 1399.

Another ghost has been reported outside the building in Castle Yard. One sighting by a lady residing opposite the yard, who observed the figure from an upstairs window, was so clear that she identified the apparition to be that of William Napier Reeve. The lady knew him well. She claims to have seen the apparition on several later occasions. The sightings were reported in the *Leicester Mail* on 19 June 1930. Another clear sighting in 1981 was of a man wearing a frock coat, stovepipe hat and holding a walking cane. William Napier Reeve seems to fit this description.

Reeve was a solicitor, author and noted historian. His passion in life was a prized collection of medals and coins. He was also very fond of this part of Leicester and wrote extensively about the castle. He died in 1888 aged seventy-seven and was buried in Bocking, Essex.

A bust of William Napier Reeve is displayed in the Leicestershire Records Office in Wigston Magna.

Castle Gateway

One of our older folklore traditions, probably not in use as much these days, would be the fiendish ploy to get energetic children in their homes and safely tucked up in bed at a civilised hour. All over England fearsome creatures would descend: in London it would be the 'Bogey Man'; Norfolk and Essex children would be in bed before the 'Marsh Man' came; in Leicester we had the 'Nine O'Clock Horses' to hide from. Sometimes though, a more terrifying creature

Castle Gateway: does Black Annis still roam this place?

would be threatened: the fearsome Black Annis.

An old hag, who wore black rags, had sharp talons and had cannibalistic tendencies, Black Annis much preferred the tender flesh of young children but would sometimes take a young lamb if desperate. Her lair was a small cave cut out of sandstone in Bower Close, Dane Hills, just west of the town. In front of the cave was a gnarled old oak tree that served as cover where she would patiently await her prey.

The eighteenth-century poet John Heyrick Jnr wrote:

Tis said the soul of mortal man recoiled
To view Black Annis's eye, so fierce and wild
Vast talons, foul with human flesh, there grew
In place of hands, and features livid blue
Glar'd in her visage; while the obscene waist
Warm sting of human victims close embraced

Just a myth of course, another story to scare the children, but perhaps like other myths and legends it has its origins in distant truth. Who is to say there was never an old hag who might have lived in a cave, wore black and had long fingernails? There has been more than one case of cannibalism recorded in England. Even a gentle old lady choosing to keep herself to herself and living in solitude might be persecuted by the ignorant and be known as 'the old witch'. Such a person was Agnes Scott, a Dominican nun. She lived as an anchorite and was described as a 'hermit of the forest'. In St Leonard's Church in leafy Swithland, a village a few miles west of Leicester, there is a small veiled statue and a brass plaque in existence. According to the inscription, Agnes was believed to have lived in a cave and tended the dying at a leper colony in Dane Hills. Needless to say she would have been ostracised by the stigma of helping the 'unclean'. She wore a black habit of that order which might also have been a basis for the legend.

The story of Black Annis concludes with her eventually being driven out of her lair. She had a tunnel to the Castle Gateway, or Rupert's Gateway as we now know it, where she remained until she was struck down with an axe. That was the end of Black Annis.

Why then do some people passing by here on summer evenings suddenly look around or look up at the structure? They have the feeling of being watched intently by 'something'. What was the blackish mist that moved rapidly into the gateway that a security guard watched from his van that was parked on Castle View? Why was a man taking photographs suddenly baffled to glimpse the back of a long black garment swishing out of sight at the wall just along the cobbles, when there had been no one around when he arrived. If it is a ghost, the blame must, of course, fall on Black Annis.

Castle Motte

As mentioned, the motte was where the original Leicester Castle stood. It is situated on Castle View behind an old pub and several cottages that are now owned by De Montfort University.

For many years the motte was inaccessible but now one may visit it through Castle Park itself. Near the Newarke end one will find a path leading up to it. A series of timber steps takes one to the summit. The motte was levelled by the Victorians to create a bowling green. As a result the

The path where footsteps were heard but no one seen.

flat surface is ideal to view the scenery from several benches that have been provided.

On a pleasant dusk in May 1992, Susan de Klerk was cycling through Castle Park. She noticed the open gateway to the motte and decided to have a look. She left her bicycle by the old stone entrance to the rear of the old Leicester Castle cellars then began the ascent. She reached the top (it is rather steep) eventually and wandered over to the other side to admire the view. Susan found the setting very tranquil and was gazing idly when she heard footsteps on gravel.

She quickly realised that the park keeper must have been coming to lock the gate. Susan then remembered that she had not bothered to lock her bicycle. She swiftly reached the first set of steps and peered over. There was no one in sight yet the sound of footsteps, which were now diminishing, were quite audible and seemed to be emanating from the gravelled path that runs level with the base of the motte and a row of iron railings leading to the rear of the old Trinity Hospital.

Susan was not particularly frightened but baffled by the incident. On reflection, Susan said she was in an almost trancelike state when she heard the sounds. Did this make her somehow more receptive to such influences?

Castle Street

I often get asked why ghosts so often seem to be of ancient figures such as Tudors, Victorians and Edwardian characters and never of more recent and ordinary persons. Well, there are, not only in the following story but I will mention the guest at the Belmont House Hotel who 'stayed' in his favourite room for three years after he died in 1990, the seventies 'hippie' who roams the old railway sidings near Station Street in Thurnby and the man who fell down a lift shaft at Wellington House in 1977.

On the corner of Castle Street and Southgate Street is a large Victorian building. It is now a call centre for a building society. It was for many years the premises of S.D. Stretton, a well-established and successful hosiery company.

In the rag trade, there used to be sayings such as, 'You can't do too much for a good gaffer' or, 'Look after the gaffer and he'll look after you'. These immortal words would be cheerily bantered about to boost moral should the dreaded term 'rush job' present itself.

In October 1972 such a situation was underway. Robert Salmon and another warehouseman were busy preparing a major rush order for dispatch. They and a number of machinists had agreed to stay late in order to have the consignment ready for the following day.

Eventually the machinists were finished, leaving only the 'boxing up' to do. This could be done early the next morning. Robert went up to the top floor to switch off any lights. Just as he went to switch the lights out he noticed a girl at the other end of the long main aisle. Robert

The old Stretton building where a ghostly 1960s 'dolly bird' still lingers.

called her to hurry up as it was getting late. He then went and switched lights off on the other work floors. Somewhat perplexed, Robert then waited on the stairs. His mate then shouted, 'Are you fit Rob, I don't know about you but I need a pint.' Robert then explained there was one more to come. 'Don't be daft, they've all gone,' replied his mate. To prove his point, Robert went up to find, and have strong words with, the young lady. To his amazement there was no one to be seen. Robert put the matter out of his mind. They locked up, left and went over to the pub.

The next day, at tea break, the mystery crept into the conversation. The fact that Robert had not recognised the girl was probably due to past situations whereby some rush jobs would involve friends or wives being 'roped in' to help with a quick dispatch. Robert had wished he had never mentioned the matter as one or two were pulling his leg. 'What did she look like then?' one of the girls piped up. Robert then described her as having short blond hair and wearing one of those short PVC coats that were popular in the sixties with white knee-high boots.

Roger, who had worked at Strettons for a good few years, then spoke of a story he had heard. Apparently in the mid-sixties a young girl working late left with some of her friends. She was halfway along Millstone Lane when she realised she had forgotten her handbag. She told her friends to carry on home. She would see them the next day. Tragically, she was run over by a car and died in hospital of her injuries.

Roger then added that there were rumours of a ghost on the top floor. Some of the women were convinced, although nothing had been seen. Robert then explained that he did not believe in ghosts, plus this person was solid, not at all as a ghost is supposed to look like.

Roger reached for his tea then sat back. 'This young girl had blond hair and a PVC coat; I think you saw her Rob.'

Newarke House Museum

This museum as we know it today was formed from two houses, Skeffington House and Wygston's Chantry House. William Wygston, a wool merchant, had the Chantry House built in 1512. The house was used by two priests to sing masses for William's soul in the Church of St Mary of the Annunciation that stood opposite. The house remained a private residence until 1940.

Skeffington House was built as a family residence in 1583 for Sir Thomas Skeffington, the High Sheriff of Leicester on three occasions. It was originally constructed of stone rubble to one storey but over the years changes were made. It was adjoined to the Chantry House in 1712. The white stucco was put on in 1790. In 1908 the properties were earmarked for factory sites. With the intervention of The Leicester Archaeological Society and Sydney Gimson, the buildings were secured for eventual use as a museum. Gimson, Chairman of Leicester Museum Committee, helped raise £3,600 for the cause. It would be forty years later that the buildings would be converted for the exhibits.

The museum is a winding place with many rooms and corridors. There is a reproduction Victorian Street complete with cobbles and a barrel organ. There is also a shoemaker's shop and a cottage that depicts what hard times this period was for some.

The clothes of 'the heaviest man in England', Daniel Lambert, are on display here. Daniel Lambert was born in Leicester on 13 March 1770. He became keeper at the County Bridewell (house of correction) that was situated on Highcross Street.

Despite his ever-increasing weight and size, he partook in various sports and was a keen

Newarke House, a historic building with a ghost or two.

hunter. In 1806 Daniel Lambert capitalised on his size by 'exhibiting himself' in a London freak show, charging five shillings a time.

He died suddenly in Stamford on 21 June 1809. Near his time of death he stood 5ft 11in high, his waist measured 9ft 4in and he weighed 52st 11lb.

Just along from the Daniel Lambert exhibits there is a large room with a Jacobean fireplace. This room is alleged to be haunted by the ghost of a small boy dressed in a Victorian era sailor suit. Apparently, he only appears to those who visit the room alone. These appearances of the child are sometimes just a flash of light caught out of the corner of the eye.

A dark, shadow-like shape has been glimpsed on one occasion. The strange figure was on the Chantry House side of a connecting doorway between the two buildings. The museum assistant who claimed to have seen it had no real fear of the apparition. This may tie in with a clerical-looking figure that was reported at the top of the main staircase, which was described as having a black cloak or long coat. An American tourist saw a dark, clerical-looking man standing outside the old doorway, he actually took a photograph and the shady figure appeared on the exposure. He gave it to one of the assistants but it mysteriously vanished. One may speculate a connection with one of the priests who were incumbent here for William Wygston.

One visitor in the Gimsom Room had an unsettling experience one afternoon. Suddenly, out of an oak-panelled wall stepped a man dressed in Elizabethan attire. The man then silently walked across the room before vanishing through an adjacent wall.

Not so long ago I visited the museum. After a pleasant stroll I spoke with two young museum assistants I had not met before. I wished to know if there had been any recent claims of ghostly phenomena. They were aware of none. One of the young ladies suggested that given the

The tree where a weird mist was witnessed.

creaking floorboards and eerie silence it would be easy for one's imagination to run riot. She did add though that on occasion there is a sensation of being observed, of not being alone.

St Mary de Castro

The church of St Mary de Castro lies on a leafy and restful corner just off Castle Street. Surprisingly, the noise and chaos from the busy St Nicholas Circle, which is only a few yards away, does not spoil the tranquillity of this pleasant scene.

Founded by Robert de Beaumont in 1107, the church was built within the fortification of Leicester Castle. Over the centuries there have been some changes made to the building. In the thirteenth century there were major works to extend the south transept with the magnificent oak-panelled ceiling; this feature has some of the finest examples of wood carving to be seen in the country. The tower and spire were added in 1400. In 1783 the spire had to be rebuilt after being destroyed by a lightning strike.

King Henry VI was knighted here in 1426 and it is alleged that Geoffrey Chaucer, author of *The Canterbury Tales*, was married in the church.

The church is reputedly haunted by a mysterious presence that seems benign. There may even be more than one phantom as descriptions vary. Interestingly, there are no recorded sightings of anything resembling the headless shadow that supposedly vanished into the porch after following the lad in the Friar Lane story. A former vicar believed there to be something of a spiritual nature about the place and seemed sympathetic to the possibility of a ghost haunting the church.

Recent experiences include two schoolgirls who ventured into the church one dinner break for a look around. They were drawn to the north aisle where a long curtain was draped. Curiosity got the better of the two girls. They slowly opened the curtains and peered in. They were suddenly startled by what looked like a white sheet dropping down before them. The pair backed off and waited for a few seconds then, unable to contain themselves, the girls had another look. There was nothing like the white sheet on the floor or anything else unusual. The schoolgirls then decided to get out of the place, in a hurry.

A cleaner was busy polishing an item of church silver in the sacristy one day when she caught sight of someone peering in through the window at her; simultaneously the door latch began to rattle. She hastily went outside and was surprised to find no one anywhere in sight. Mystified she went back inside. Although she only had a quick look at the face, it was long enough to see that it was hooded and had a greenish haze, like an aura.

A young couple who had worked late into the night to assist with a function at a dance academy were the next people to have an odd experience. They decided to visit a Chinese takeaway then sit on one of the several benches that are positioned at the foot of Castle Street near to the old Tudor Gateway and part of the churchyard of St Mary's. They were quite alone and were idly chatting when they both noticed a change in the atmosphere. A tangible sensation of oppressiveness in the air like a heavy thunderstorm was brewing. Then a greyish mist was seen to form by a large oak tree that has a long branch supported by a timber stanchion. The mist was quite shapeless and vague, almost like cigarette smoke. They both watched intently, wondering what would happen next. After about a minute, the mist simply dissipated. Shortly after, the oppressive atmosphere seemed to fade. The young man found it interesting but his partner was less than enthusiastic about staying so they left the area.

FOUR

OLD BELGRAVE

B elgrave is a very busy, thriving area, unique in that it has retained its village atmosphere. A particularly pleasant way to visit is to follow the river from Abbey Park and just meander until you are there.

The heart of Belgrave is the area of Church Road, Thurcaston Road and Vicarage Lane. The busy Loughborough Road has no effect on the tranquillity of the place and is almost as if one is out in the countryside.

The Belgravians were a very close-knit community at one time. If there had been a misdemeanour in the village and the miscreant was a local, it would be highly unlikely that the culprit would be brought to book. In the early 1900s one of the more popular forms of recreation for the men would be the little gambling schools. In summer they would meet up around the fields by the river for a few rounds of 'pitch and toss', a simple game where players would place some pennies either heads or tails up, the 'chucker' would throw a penny and whatever side it landed was the winner. The constabulary took a dim view of such practices, however. One memorable Friday evening, a notoriously keen police inspector crept up on a small party. He appeared and declared, 'I've got you now'. The men did no more than throw the furious policeman into the river. The next day when enquires were launched to track down the culprits, no one knew anything. As a result, Belgrave earned another title, 'Dummy Town'. Any trouble, everyone was struck dumb.

The police inspector did not drown but managed to clamber out, so it is not he who haunts the area and road around the old toll bridge. So who is it? A taxi driver told me that more than a few cabbies cutting along Thurcaston Road in the early hours have slowed down near the bridge because of a man wandering all over the road, as if drunk or in distress, who then somehow just moves out of sight into nothing. He is just one of a bunch of spectral characters that are reputed to linger around this enigmatic little place.

Belgrave Hall

Belgrave Hall was built in 1709 for Edmund and Anne Cradock. Edmund unfortunately died shortly after taking occupancy. In 1771 the hall was then bought by John and Helen Simmons with whom it stayed until 1767. William Southwell then took the house for his brother-in-law, William Vann. The Vann's ran a successful hosiery business from the house using the stables and some of the other outbuildings. Many local framework knitters were employed here.

John Ellis was born in 1789. After many years living and working on Beaumont Leys Farm he decided he wanted a larger home. He had learned of a coal seam in north-west Leicester and encouraged George Stephenson of the Leicester & Swannington Railway to lay a line through, as this cheap source of coal would bring prosperity to Leicester. He later became chairman of

Belgrave Hall; a ghost known as the Terracotta Lady lingers here to this day.

the Midland County Railway. In 1848 he stood for Parliament and was duly elected. Up until his death in 1862 John Ellis worked tirelessly and achieved much success in the business world. In 1847 John Ellis and his family went to view Belgrave Hall. He was very taken by the place. One of his daughters, Eliza, commented on the place being ghostly, the white hall and staircase having a ghostly hue to it. John's brother William and John Ellis's six daughters resided at Belgrave Hall until the last daughter, Mary, died in 1923.

After another family who had done well in the hosiery trade, the Morleys, took the house, the building was later purchased by the Leicester Corporation in 1936 for use as a period museum.

Belgrave Hall and its gardens are almost like having a little stately home to wander. It has a feel to it as if the entire family have gone out and the visitor is viewing an empty house. The tantalising aroma of baked bread and other delights are sometimes noticed wafting through the building. Is this the work of the 'Terracotta Lady'? If it is, no one is complaining. None of the staff have a problem with this benign presence that occasionally wanders around. Some have become quite used to hearing dainty footsteps on the polished floorboards of the first-floor landing when no visitors are up there. One member of staff commented, 'a house like this should have its ghosts'. There are rare instances of blasts of cold air, as experienced many years ago by museum assistant John Postle in the music room and more recently by two assistants who experienced a cold spot so severe that they saw their own breath hang in the air.

Tom Smith is a huge man. After a spell in the Coldstream Guards he joined the Museum Service in 1982. He worked at the main museum and art gallery in New Walk for a while then

Above left: *The stairs on which the ghost momentarily appeared to Mike the gardener.*

Above right: *Charlotte Ellis, a formidable character perhaps unwilling to depart her beloved home.*

asked to be moved to Belgrave Hall, as it was quieter. Eventually his wish was granted. Tom liked the culture at Belgrave Hall. He was soon told of the ghost but took no notice, 'I don't believe in such poppycock'. However, this was to change on one very dark and gloomy winter morning. It was customary on the early shift to arrive around 7.00 a.m. Tom would let himself in, then the priority was to put the kettle on. Next the shutters were removed and coal fires prepared for whatever room would be needed. Fires were lit on a rota basis. On his return to the old kitchen, Tom suddenly felt an odd sensation, like an electric charge in the air. He looked around but saw nothing. Then an awful sensation of pure terror set in; Tom's hair literally stood on end as he stopped rigid, wondering what would happen next. The sensation then simply ceased. Tom, somewhat shaken, went back to the kitchen to sit down and recover from whatever it was. 'I don't know what it was but I never want to go through that again,' Tom stated.

Sightings are rare indeed. In early 1998 there were two brief ghostly appearances. Assistant Jeanie Bilton had almost reached the top of the stairs to the first floor when she glimpsed a pair of legs that vanished as she looked over, also a large item of furniture with which she was unfamiliar disappeared with the legs.

Late one afternoon, Mike the gardener was engaged in some idle chat in the main hallway when he caught out of the corner of his eye someone on the stairs. He glanced up and stared at a lady of advancing years, wearing a terracotta-coloured dress and black boots. She looked right through him as if he was not there then vanished. The vision appeared solid and lasted for just three or four seconds.

In December of that year an unexplained image appeared outside which was caught on a CCTV camera during the night. It was discovered during routine checks of security cameras by one of the museum assistants. It was initially thought to be an intruder. The curator, Mr Warburton, examined the footage then had it looked at by a security consultant. It was not an intruder. Had something supernatural been captured on film?

As Mr Warburton was of a scientific background this would be an opportunity to find out once and for all if there was indeed anything in these claims of a ghost haunting Belgrave Hall.

Over the coming months, many experts from the world of parapsychology visited to examine the footage. Dr Alan Gauld from Nottingham University conducted a study and concluded that the image was of a banking owl. Mr Maurice Grosse, Chairman of the Spontaneous Cases Committee of the Society for Psychical Research, found the image of interest but not proof of an apparition. American experts Dr Larry Montz and Daena Smoller carried out an in-depth study. Their hypothesis was that the image was merely a glitch. Daena did add that there were mild forms of spiritual activity in the building. Other suggestions were that the image was a bat, an oak leaf or simply a raindrop. To this day the matter remains unresolved.

Ghost research seems to indicate that in instances where an apparition can be identified, the person was in life of a certain character, stubborn, forceful and determined. 'Women's Lib' as it was called is assumed to be part of the 'swinging sixties' culture but such equality was fought for during the mid-eighteenth century also. Just the mere mention of the word 'woman' would cause gentlemen to turn red with fury and splutter into their brandy glasses at a dozen Pall Mall clubs. It was time for change.

Women's suffrage had not been taken seriously for decades. Eventually something had to give, and it did. A suffragette rally in the capital became so riotous that nearly 200 women were arrested. Later actions were little short of complete anarchy. Train seats were slashed, bricks were thrown through windows at the Palace of Westminster, sports pavilions were burnt down and bombs were placed near the Bank of England. One leading suffragette, Emily Davison, killed herself by throwing herself under the King's racehorse.

Charlotte Ellis was another leading suffragette. A staunch figure, sometimes outspoken, she was nearly imprisoned after her public outcry against compulsory vaccinations that were killing more people than doing any good. She was also a Quaker and lived at Belgrave Hall for her entire life. Charlotte was very attached to the hall and has long been assumed to be its ghost. She is not always to be found in the hall but out in the gardens of which she was very fond. She may have been responsible for a recent incident that was both frightening and frustrating for the witness. At dusk in early 2004 a young lady was in the gardens filming with a video camera. After she was satisfied she turned the thing off. Then, out of nowhere, a white column of concentrated mist glided in front of her then dissipated in seconds. If only she had carried on filming!

St Peter's Church

St Peter's is a fine old church which originates from the eleventh century. It has the most magnificent Norman doorway in England. The adjacent vicarage was demolished in the late 1960s. There have, for several years, been reports of an unsettling atmosphere around the churchyard.

If anyone would haunt this tranquil place it would be one Joseph Cave, an eccentric character if ever there was. He had the morbid desire for his tombstone to be erected nine years before his death. He was very methodical and despised things being done in a hasty manner. Joseph liked to be one step ahead.

When he decided to have his grave dug, he came over to the churchyard and oversaw the task. When the hole was dug and clay pipes lit he joined the two labourers for a cheerful rendering of 'Poor Old Joe'. He was laid to rest on 6 August 1921, his weathered tombstone bearing fresh inscription.

However, unless Joseph was laid to rest wearing a long grey dress, we must assume the apparition seen in the churchyard by a former landlady of the Talbot and two locals to be that of a woman. Some think it may be one of the Ellis sisters, Sarah Jane, who is interred here.

The Talbot Inn

There is thought to have been a house on this site since the twelfth century. Inspections of parts of the cellar by archaeologists confirm this. During the years when it was a coaching inn, the locals would have sneered upon the wretches brought here for a last meal before being taken to Red Hill where the gallows stood. A few of them would then have followed the cart and joined the rabble to see the terrible spectacle before coming back for more ale.

There was a small brew house at the rear. Not only would ale be brewed for the Talbot but also many of the inns in the area. The kegs and pins would have been distributed on a horse-drawn cart by a hefty fellow and a lad making a few coppers and a tip as was the tradition. Often the tip was ale, so the horse was often left to find its own way!

The church owned the inn at one time. The revenue from rent would go toward the upkeep of the church and the nearby toll bridge.

The earliest recorded hosts were Henry and Mary Dawson. Mary was a feisty woman indeed. God help anyone who crossed her. Sadly she perished during the difficult labour of her sixth child. She returns to the pub now and again and is easily recognisable with her lovely flowing hair.

A strange shimmering figure was observed out in the car park some years ago. The landlady, who was tending some border plants, suddenly felt freezing cold. She looked up from what she was doing and was startled to see a hazy figure of a small man with a shimmering aura. The man remained perfectly still for several seconds then dissipated leaving one very terrified landlady. This vision may have been one of the many vagabonds brought back from the gallows to the little mortuary. Early forms of medical experiments were carried out on the fresh bodies of convicted murderers here. This small building in the car park is now used as a garage.

After a terrible fire in the late 1950s the top storey of the inn was removed. Other alterations were carried out; the old bar is now the lounge, the stables have gone and more entrances have been created. This might explain the mysterious fellow who walks through a wall. The man forms

Left: *The Talbot Inn, an old coaching house with some dark secrets.*

Below: *The old mortuary where the bodies of hung murderers were unceremoniously dissected for medical research.*

in the bar near the pool table. He has a cape raincoat reminiscent of the type in fashion around the 1930s. Apparently he has a leather purse that he peers into, then he turns and strolls through the wall to his left, along the old off sales and into the lounge. Where he walks was originally an entrance door. It would seem he has no knowledge of this as he is in another dimension.

A mischievous small boy may be responsible for moving balls about on the pool table and bad attempts at playing the 'horses' teeth', the upright piano. He has only been seen twice, once in the cellar and then in the lounge where he sat on a stool swinging his legs vigorously. He smiled at the barmaid but vanished as she walked over to him.

The present hosts, Sharon and Robert, have had no ghostly experiences themselves since taking the pub in 2001. Perhaps time will tell.

Victorian Pumping Station

Just over the old toll bridge to the west lies the Abbey Pumping Station, a grim, foreboding-looking building.

It stands in the shadow of the futuristic National Space Centre. This structure is mainly of transparent plastic sheeting; quite a few refer to it as resembling a blown-up plastic bag! It is surreal to view a Victorian and a space-age building side by side.

The pumping station was built in 1891. It would pump sewage to the treatment works at Beaumont Leys until its closure in 1964. After an interim period the building was re-opened as a museum of technology. It is also a paradise for steam enthusiasts. A team of dedicated volunteers with boundless enthusiasm assist with restoration and upkeep of not only the huge beam engines, but also other steam-driven machines.

In civil engineering around the 1800s, tragedy was all too common. Many a workman died a nasty death on many building projects. Sometimes a black brick would be laid in memory of an unfortunate builder. The Forth Bridge must hold the record for most lives lost on a construction, as a total of eighty men perished.

One workman was killed during the construction of the pumping station. He fell 50ft from the top balcony onto one of the huge beam engines in the pump house and his ghost is said to linger, particularly around the engine room. One staff member often claimed to be intimidated if locking up by himself. Nothing has ever been seen but there is a slight presence sensed.

Lindsey Boyes and his wife, Doris, visited the building during an exhibition of the science and history of moving pictures from 1800 to 1895. Lindsey is a keen film enthusiast and is fascinated by the origins of the moving image. 'What the butler saw' machines, 'nickleodeons' and lanterns were on display. They were both idly examining an ancient projector when their attention was diverted to one of these devices that give the illusion of movement; a cylinder with several silhouettes of a man in various positions – when the cylinder turns the man appears to move. Well, it was moving. In fact it was moving very vigorously. They both stared at the machine then moved closer to it; the thing was operated by turning a handle, manually. They stood laughing at the display then it abruptly ceased. Lindsay declined to mention anything to any of the staff. It was three years later that Lindsey found out about the ghostly engineer. Well, it must have been him!

The Steam Museum. Its construction cost the life of one man.

FIVE

GALLERY OF GHOSTS

Abbey Park

Is it merely pleasant nostalgia, or was the British summer of times past, long, hot and pleasant? It always seemed so. Some of my happiest memories as a child were the visits to Abbey Park, where one could spend an entire day. The feeding of the ducks, the model yachts on the lake, the smell of baking bread wafting over from Frears Bakery on Abbey Lane. Then there were the obligatory ice cream cornets and flailing with fishing nets that never seemed to catch anything. Simple pleasures really.

The park opened in 1882. The fifty-two acres of land was a focal point for the Victorians. They would sit under the weeping willows on the sloping banks of the River Soar idly watching the world go by with the occasional excitement as a clumsy attempt at punting would result in someone getting wet. On Sundays the stirring brass band tones would seep over from the bandstand as picnics were consumed.

For decades the park was the setting for the City of Leicester Show or the 'Abbey Park Show' as locals dubbed the event. It was held annually on the August Bank Holiday. There were dog shows, marquees with horticultural exhibits, the ever well-attended beer tent and all manner of things to see and do.

Little has changed. The menagerie is still there with its rabbits, goats and meowing peacocks. The menagerie stands in the shadow of the abbey ruins. The abbey was founded by the Earl of Leicester, Robert le Bossa, in 1132 and closed during the dissolution in 1538. In 1613, William Cavendish, the first Earl of Devonshire, bought the property. He called it Cavendish House. Charles I took the house after the siege of Leicester in 1645. On his departure he ordered that the place be razed to the ground.

On a pleasant sunny morning in the mid-1970s the gardeners were busy out on the park. One gardener was engaged in his work when he became aware of someone standing close by. He looked up to see a man standing before him. The man was dressed in a rich velvet very short jacket, doublet-type breeches with hose stockings. He also had a white lace neck ruff that suggested his costume to be late Tudor or early Elizabethan. The gardener listened as the man spoke and gestured enthusiastically about Cavendish House, which they were both adjacent to. The gardener, although somewhat flummoxed, assumed the man to be part of some pageant or maybe an actor attached to a re-enactment group such as the Sealed Knot Society. It was only when the man promptly vanished that the shock set in.

The shaken gardener told the park superintendent, John Darlow, of the incident. Mr Darlow listened and seemed sympathetic to the report, taking it quite seriously. This might have been due to the lodge built into to the ruins in which Mr Darlow resided having a reputation of being haunted by a figure from the Tudor or Elizabethan period. Perhaps this was the ghost of William Cavendish.

The ruins of Cavendish House.

The old lodge, now deserted – well maybe.

Asfordby Street Policing Unit

Fire-fighters are a breed apart, brave, unflinching and dedicated. If they're not balancing off a tree branch to rescue a cat they will be at the scene of a nasty car accident or raging fire.

Asfordby Street Fire Station opened in 1899. In those days the tender would have been drawn by one of the two shire horses who grazed on a small field opposite.

By the 1930s, an open cab, petrol-driven Dennis fire engine was in use. The 'Fire Bobbies' would have worn a collarless shirt, waistcoat and a reefer-type serge coat. The helmet would have been stiff leather and cork. The earlier brass helmets, although being very stout, were heavy and found to be dangerous where electricity may have been involved. Many of the men lived on the premises whilst others resided nearby in several terraced houses. The station officer, Abraham Hincks, was a man to be feared. Life in a fire station was very disciplined indeed and God help anyone who incurred the wrath of the station officer.

Although feared, he would have cared about his men and their welfare. His quarters occupied a large area of the first floor with an office, living room, bathroom and bedroom. Shortly after being measured up for a new uniform, Abraham Hincks collapsed and died of a major heart attack in February 1937.

A few years later, rumours of a ghost began to circulate around the station. Firemen are keen practical jokers and would have played up to this opportunity. But this notion was not just a folly; there had been several definite glimpses of a shadowy figure near the station officer's quarters. Eventually the ghost was dubbed 'Abe', something no one would have dared call Station Officer Hincks in life.

A former fire officer, Trevor Edwards, was stationed at Asfordby Street and remembered an incident when he was in the mess room above the old hayloft. He was watching the television late one evening when he received a poke in the back, he looked around but there was no one there.

In 1973, the building ceased to be a fire station. A brand new building on Hastings Road was ready and would house the appliances and the three watches of the Leicester Fire Service Eastern Division. The building would become a police station. The major move was underway.

There has always been a culture of lightweight sparring between the services so as the police were moving in they would have been cheerfully told of the various quirks of the building and of the ghost to which, I dare say, little heed would have been paid.

There were rare instances of a cold, unsettling sensation around the upper portion of the small staircase that led to the living quarters and occasions when persons in the vicinity of the haunted rooms felt they were being watched.

Shortly after the building was converted to a police station, an evening cleaner complained of hearing voices and unexplained footsteps on the old small staircase. The cleaner knew all the staff in that part of the building had left, so who was it?

The most dramatic incident to date involved a young PC attached to the Central Traffic Division. The PC arrived at the building just before midnight when his shift would finish. He parked his vehicle in the bay at the rear and let himself in. He then went up the back stairs to leave his report log sheet, as was normal procedure. There was suddenly a loud bang from the next landing up. The PC, with caution, ascended the stairs to the report writing room from where the noise seemed to have emanated. He entered and looked around the room; there was no one there at all. The atmosphere then rapidly changed and the temperature plummeted. His police training had certainly not prepared him for anything of this nature. Then the door behind him slammed shut with considerable force. The PC wrenched it open and ran down the stairs in record time.

At the present time, things are quiet. There are still a few, though unwilling to admit it, who are not too enthusiastic about venturing near the old fire station officer's rooms alone.

Blackfriars Hall

Blackfriars Hall was originally the old Holy Cross Church and Priory, the first building to be erected on New Walk in 1818. New Walk is a unique, three-quarter-mile long pedestrian promenade that starts at Welford Place and finishes at Granville Road.

Father Norbert Wylie, a man of great integrity, was a prior here at the time of the First World War. He was devoted to his work and religious convictions. He was also fondly recalled for his devotion to those in poor health. The ghost of a cleric has been reported on numerous occasions. The features were so well defined that the apparition was identified as Father Norbert Wylie. The figure was seen to approach the altar in preparation to taking Holy Communion to a sick person.

There is also said to be a former prior who silently moves about the place then just vanishes. Elliot O' Donnell, that most intrepid of ghost hunters, makes reference to this in his volume *Haunted Churches*. He spent a night in the priory in 1929, but unfortunately he experienced absolutely nothing.

Blackfriars Hall. Two religious figures, long dead, choose to return here.

A Mr Paul Brown and a couple of his workmates might have unknowingly had a ghostly encounter. Blackfriars Hall has a youth club. In the early 1980s, a few young workers from a nearby roofing company, Duplus Domes Ltd, were allowed access to the hall for occasional lunchtime games of five-a-side football. This access eventually came to an end as these games usually occurred after a hasty beer or two in a nearby pub and often involved steel toe-capped boots on the polished wooden floor, colourful language and shouting.

I knew Mr Brown well, he told me of having a semi-drunken game and having to curb the 'effing and blinding' because of the monk passing through. It must have been the monk who moaned about them that got their drunken sporting activities stopped. There are no monks here now, though of course there used to be.

New Walk is supposed to be for pedestrians only, though occasionally cyclists flaunt this idea and there has been more than one bruised shin and cracked rib. A young man, Jim Nicholls, would often use this thoroughfare to cycle down if he was late for work. It was about 7.15 a.m., just as it was starting to get light, in mid-February 1988. He was about to turn off New Walk onto Park Street when he noticed a mysterious man on the grass outside the church wearing cream robes. Jim looked in casual interest then carried on.

Six years later he and his girlfriend attended a guided ghost walk. After the guide had told the group of the ghosts here, Jim pondered. He had cycled down New Walk many times at often around the same time of day. He had never noticed a priest before and why would a clergyman be in full regalia at such an early hour?

Church Gate

A pub on Church Gate has endured occasional supernatural trouble in the time-honoured tradition of glasses falling off shelves, mysterious sounds and unnatural, icy draughts.

The pub has had an average succession of couples running the business. Some have felt there to be something odd about the place whilst others have enjoyed a normal period of tenure with nothing unusual whatsoever.

The pub has had several names and it was during the period when it was called the Long Stop that there was quite a notable barrage of ghostly activity over a short period. One evening in 1976 two bar staff noticed a shadowy person who just seemed to come from nowhere. They watched in disbelief as the person moved over to a corner of a room and disappeared. A few days later, the landlady confronted a shapeless, undulating mist whilst down in the cellar. Later on in the evening a similar effect appeared from nowhere, glided along behind the bar then dissipated at the doorway to the cellar. This mist was seen by the landlord and, I was told, a well-known radio and television personality who was having a quiet drink at the bar before appearing at the nearby Bailey's nightclub.

Intrigued by the strange, misty shape, the landlady decided to do some digging into the history of the place. It eventually came to light that in October 1896 a man died suddenly on the premises. Then it was discovered during a spiritualist séance in the north of England that a man called Harry Staines, a previous landlord, wished it to be known that he had fallen down the cellar steps and died as a result. The spiritualist carefully collated the information then compiled a letter to the pub. The landlady was understandably astonished when she read the letter. In effect, the ghost had helped her to find out who he was.

The resting place of Harry Staines — but does he rest?

The old Freewheeler building.

Also on Church Gate, right at the other end, stands another building with a haunted history. The sightings and experiences were most prevalent during the period the building was a dancehall, the Freewheeler. The lounge, main bar area and dance floor took up the entire ground floor. Toilets were on the first-floor landing. The remainder of this and the upper floor was used for storage rooms, offices, etc.

One Saturday night in 1975 a group of people were sitting around a large table chatting away and relaxing. Then, over a long period, four of the girls in the party became withdrawn, almost trancelike. After a while two of the girls became quite upset for some reason and started crying; others in the group, clearly embarrassed, tried to calm them down and ask what the problem was. The two tearful girls then decided to go upstairs to the toilets to clean up and re-apply their make-up.

When they arrived on the landing, the two girls felt an urge to go up the other stairs as if 'drawn by something'. As they were about to ascend the staircase, the girls were suddenly prevented from doing so by a large man, dressed in a black dinner jacket and a bow tie; he was the doorman. He kindly but firmly refused to let them go up. One of the girls, Jane, asked the man what was up there. The doorman simply said, 'You don't want to go up there love'. It seemed as if the doorman knew something but wished not to elaborate and that this was not the first time such an incident had occurred.

The girls then freshened up, went down and joined the rest of the group, where the other two girls had also cheered up. They then enjoyed the rest of the evening as if nothing had happened.

A local musician told me that he had no doubt that there was sometimes a peculiar atmosphere about parts of the building. He could not say it to be a ghost as such, but certainly not a result of too much alcohol!

One room in particular was thought to harbour some kind of discarnate presence. This room is on the top floor. Late one evening, a barmaid was asked to go and collect something from the room. She was only too well aware of the rumours and with mild trepidation went upstairs. She opened the door, switched on the light and was horrified to see what looked like a face forming among the pendants of a chandelier. She screamed and ran back downstairs.

One barman claimed to have confronted the figure of an old man on several occasions. The sightings always occurred around the upper landings. The figure would be stock-still. He had a frock coat and a cravat held in place by a large gold pin and both hands would rest on a walking cane. The figure had a very neat beard and carried an expression of pure malevolence.

The ghostly sightings may or may not have something to do with the building being used as a mortuary at one time.

Crescent

The Crescent on King Street was built by Alderman James Rawson in 1826. The three-storey building containing fourteen houses was for many years home to some of Leicester's most well-to-do people: Edward L. Stephens who designed the grandstand at Leicester Racecourse, the

The Crescent where a ghostly trio still linger on.

artist George S. Elgood, Henry Morgan and Samuel Squire who founded the department store on Market Street (now Waterstones) to name but a few.

The Crescent remained in the Rawson family until 1920. A Mr Arthur Wakeley then bought two of the houses. The purchase included the remaining pillar of the High Cross that the son of James Rawson had placed in the garden as reclamation from Highcross Street in 1836. This piece of stone can now be seen in Cheapside.

Over the years, many of the houses were converted into flats or offices. In the early 1960s The Crescent became under threat of the bulldozer as planning for the ever-increasing volume of road traffic meant the proposed ring road would go straight through it. Thankfully The Crescent survived as planners worked out an alternative route. Today, The Crescent is occupied by various businesses. To have an address here is indeed a sign of prestige.

There are claimed to be three separate phantoms inhabiting three of the houses, or were, as there are no recent reports of anything untoward. One manifestation came in the form of a malevolent build-up of oppressive energy with a freezing atmosphere. It lasted for only seconds but left those in its wake feeling deeply disturbed. The second ghost was that of an old lady. This apparition exuded a feeling of wellbeing. She seemed aware of those who beheld her and smiled at them. The third ghost was a scruffy looking, rustic old fellow. He had long grey hair and a beard. He was apparently of an unpleasant nature. A man committed suicide here by hanging himself from a stair banister, which may account for the latter of the trio.

Fish Market

Ghosts, it seems, do not always appear alone. There have been claims of people finding themselves experiencing an entire past vision. One such incident was reported in December 1993.

Alan Jones was meandering around the first-floor gallery of the indoor market that overlooks the fish and poultry stalls. He had just left a large stall that sold foam rubber and various fabrics and turned through a doorway then descended a staircase.

He then found himself in what looked like a large fish hall. The place seemed deserted and eerily quiet. Alan found the place very dirty and through grimy windows he looked over rooftops that did not appear familiar at all.

Something told him to keep going. He saw a figure glaring at him as he moved towards a staircase. He was then in the normal fish market on the ground floor. Completely dazed and confused, Alan collected his thoughts; the experience had lasted just seconds but seemed a lot longer. He left the market and went home.

It was later established that the staircase that Alan claimed to descend does not exist. There is a corridor with various offices for market inspectors, administration and sundry areas for storage, etc.

A pub called the White Swan and a small shopping arcade once occupied the area where the alleged incident occurred. The original fish and poultry market was situated a hundred yards away on the other side of the road.

A baffling mystery; such incidents reported as this are called 'timeslips'.

Friars Mills

Leicester has its fair share of factory sites. The oldest factory is that of Donisthorpe Ltd, who for two centuries have been involved in the dyeing of wool, textiles and fabrics. The building, on the banks of the River Soar, is said to stand on the site of an ancient monastery, hence being called Friars Mills.

Several workers have met the phantom friar. Often, early morning cleaners would catch a fleeting glimpse of a dark shadow appearing and disappearing around the offices. One lady felt so intimidated, she flatly refused to work in certain areas alone.

Ex-employee Keith Bindley spoke of an instance in 1971 where he experienced something of a ghostly nature. It was on a lunchtime break; Keith was alone sitting down in the cotton polishing room with his flask and sandwiches to hand, idly scanning a magazine on his chosen hobby, bird watching. The quiet was then disturbed by a succession of faint tapping noises. Keith listened for a while then it stopped. He then picked up his magazine and shook his head. Shortly the noise began again. Keith got up and looked around the large area then on the wide aisle he was surprised to see several wooden cotton bobbins scattered on the stone, cobbled floor. These bobbins were earlier stacked in a wicker trolley some 40 yards away. The other incident was in the same area but at a different time of day, around 9.30 p.m. Again, Keith was alone. He was collecting a number of cardboard cartons to assemble when he felt the temperature drop quite rapidly. He looked around fully expecting to see a ghost but there was nothing there. Then a

Friars Mills: a harmless former prior still returns here.

feeling of dread seemed to permeate the atmosphere, this slowly intensified. Keith felt his hair start to lift and that was enough – he ran out of the room and down the stairs with considerable gusto.

Another incident occurred when a nightwatchman was out in the yard in the early hours with his Alsatian dog. Everything was routine until they were right over near the river wall. The dog then froze, refusing to budge. Its hackles then went up. The nightwatchman shone his torch around but saw nothing to account for the dog acting up. He then had to literally drag the dog along by the wall. The animal was looking intently at something the man was unaware of. After moving a few yards further along, the dog reacted normally.

On another occasion out in the yard, a worker went over to an old stone structure known as 'the penance cell', which was used for storage. The worker went inside and, in his words, 'It was like walking into a freezer, you could have frozen a slab of butter in there.' Then just to his left he saw someone. It was dark but light enough to note a brownish garment like robes with a low sagging hood as if the head was bowed. The man ran out and excitedly called one of his colleagues over. He told him what he had seen. They both then went over and very slowly peered inside. The air temperature felt normal and there was nothing untoward in the storage building.

BBC Radio Leicester did a small feature on the building and its ghost. The outside broadcast unit arrived, the gateman showed them where to park then a preliminary tour of the building was arranged. At around halfway around the tour the sound engineer was amazed to discover his recording machine was running, he had not even set it up at this stage.

In 1924, during excavations on the site, a skeleton was unearthed which some consider to be the cause of the minor disturbances and appearance of the harmless prior.

Frog Island

This part of Leicester was known as Frogmire in medieval times. As the town expanded, houses were needed. Row upon row of 'two-up, two-down' dwellings spread outwards to Hinckley Road, Fosse Road and Woodgate (so-called because wood from Leicester Forest was brought here and sold). Slowly the community increased with shops, factories and pubs.

Today, the terraces remain, three of the pubs have gone, the Cricketers Rest, the Friar Tuck and the Robin Hood. At the time of writing much of the industrial part of Frog Island is being chewed away by large machines, like mechanical dinosaurs, as part of a vast redevelopment project. The shops on Woodgate are thriving in what has now become a fashionable area to live, terraced houses reaching ridiculously high prices.

Of the many hosiery firms in the area, Britella Ltd was one of the largest and was situated on New Pingle Street. Claims of a ghost causing havoc in the factory started to be reported in the late 1960s; the unseen menace unsettled so many staff that at one stage a strike was threatened.

Eventually it was decided something had to be done. In 1970 an archdeacon from Loughborough conducted an exorcism on the site that seemed to be a success, with only minor reports filtering through of any spectral activity.

Late one night in the early 1980s, a police constable was dispatched to the area to investigate as a burglar alarm had been activated. The panda car arrived and pulled over on the private slip-road. The officer got out of the vehicle and began checking the yards adjacent to the buildings. He then spied the silhouette of a person moving across the yard. He assumed it to be a nightwatchman or even an intruder. The constable approached the figure, who seemed impervious to what was happening. He shouted over and trained his flashlight on the figure, who simply disappeared.

Such incidents are not uncommon in the police service. The majority are never entered into notebooks or incident reports simply because the witness will be the butt of jokes from colleagues for a considerable period.

Next to the bridge over the Grand Union Canal stands the North Bridge Tavern, built just after the navigation was cut. It has served as a welcome stop for bargees and of course many factory workers over the years. The pub has a resident ghost, 'the Pink Lady', who, it is believed, came about after Ouija board sessions on the site in the early 1980s.

In April 1992, a company involved in the manufacture of belts and braces moved into premises adjacent to the pub that had remained empty for some time. In October, the first of several reports were made to the management of strange goings on. Unexplained cracking sounds, infra-red alarm systems malfunctioning, faint breezes similar to the sensation of being passed by someone in close proximity, footsteps in empty rooms and a sighting of a hazy pink apparition. The majority of these incidents occurred around 3.00 p.m.

Renowned psychic investigator, Rita Goold, was called it to see if she could throw any light on the mystery. After spending many hours in the building she only reported a few clicking sounds, unfortunately nothing conducive was forthcoming.

It then later seemed that the resident ghost of the pub had 'defected' to the factory. Several months of minor disturbances continued before slowly ceasing. Then the ghost 'returned' to its usual place, showing its might by leaving a full, eleven-gallon beer barrel on a high timber strut in the cellar. The factory was glad to be rid of it and the pub was pleased to have its Pink Lady where she belonged.

Frog Island is on a ley line. These straight lines are thought to be remains of ancient holy tracks. Many believe these lines channel mystical earth energies. The term 'ley' was originated by Alfred Watkins, whose book, *The Old Straight Track*, is considered as the bible of enthusiasts and ley hunters. Watkins extensive' research established that ley lines are linked to sites such as ancient earthworks, hilltops, stone circles, mottes, religious places and standing stones.

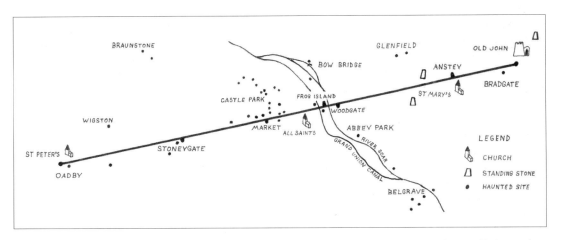

The Leicester ley line, all the sites in Haunted Leicester *are marked out. (One must judge for oneself what might constitute 'on' or 'near').*

Lady Jane Grey, a tragic figure who is said to haunt the bleak remains of her former home.

What has this to do with ghosts? Well, a popular theory is that ley lines are a 'focus area' for paranormal phenomena. Enduring hauntings and apparitions seem most prominent on or near to these lines, particularly where they cross

Leicester has such a line running through it. The line starts at St Peter's Church in Oadby, passing through Stoneygate, part of the marketplace, Cank Street, Highcross Street, All Saint's Church, Frog Island (as mentioned), the village of Anstey where a standing stone exists, and finishing near 'Old John' in Bradgate Park. This stone folly was built as a result of a tragic accident. A windmill used to exist on the hill that was destroyed by fire in 1778. The miller, Old John, survived by doing odd jobs here and there to earn a living. In 1786, the fifth Earl of Stamford wanted a huge beacon lit on the hill to mark the occasion of his son's coming of age celebrations. Old John was given the task.

The old miller over several days gathered logs, tar barrels and whatever else he could find and built the huge bonfire. At dusk on the night of the celebration the fire was lit. When the fire was at its fiercest, the whole thing collapsed, fatally injuring the old miller.

As a memorial to the much-loved old man, a folly was erected and, befitting of Old John's passion for beer, the structure was shaped like an ale tankard. Old John looks over the town and is thought of by many as a familiar old friend.

While in Bradgate, mention must be made of that most enduring local figure, Lady Jane Grey. She had a happy childhood at Bradgate House, where she partook in sewing, her love of poetry, Latin, religious study and her happy times with tutor John Aylsham. If distraught she would visit the hexagonal tower where she would often simply just look out over the beautiful parkland. She left Bradgate when she was nine years old. Seven years later Jane became ensnarled in the Tudor power struggles. The Duke of Northumberland knew that if Mary Tudor should succeed the ailing King Edward VI, his days would have been numbered. He hatched a plot to thwart this possibility. He bribed Jane's parents, the Duke and Duchess of Suffolk, to force her to marry his son, Lord Guilford Dudley. As Jane was in line for the throne, his son would be King. Jane had no desire to marry or become Queen but had to obey her parents.

After the death of the King, Jane was proclaimed Queen on 10 July 1553. Mary pressed her claim to the throne. Northumberland opposed her but lost the resulting battle. Mary was proclaimed the rightful heir to the throne. Jane was happy to relinquish her title but she was convicted of treason and incarcerated in the Bloody Tower at the Tower of London. Here she was treated reasonably but the spectre of death hung over her. She must have yearned for her simple and innocent life at Bradgate and according to history she defiantly vowed to return to her former home shortly before she was beheaded on 13 February 1554.

On the dawn of the fateful day, Jane was led to the green next to the White Tower carrying her prayer book. She asked the dean of St Paul's if she may read the psalm of *Miserere mei Deus* and this wish was granted. Her gown was then removed. With her dignity still intact she kneeled down on the straw. The executioner asked for her forgiveness, Jane nodded and asked that he dispatch her quickly. A white handkerchief was placed over her eyes then her head guided onto the block. Her last words were: 'Lord, into thy hands I command my spirit.' She was only sixteen.

Some believe that Lady Jane Grey has returned. Sometimes an eerie sensation is sensed around parts of the lonely ruins of Bradgate House, particularly the old hexagonal tower. Dark shadows flitting about and a hovering column of grey-blue mist have also been seen at night near the old chapel. Some claim that her ghost is taken in a coach drawn by four horses from Bradgate House to the little church at Newtown Linford for midnight mass every Christmas Eve. I know of no sightings, but the sound of galloping horses and the creak and rattle of a carriage has been supposedly heard twice.

Lady Jane Grey may not be alone in her ghostly perambulations in this magnificent deer park. A monk appeared in a photograph taken on the little bridge over the River Lyn; a rustic looking fellow with long hair tied back in a ponytail and with a leather eye patch stormed through a wall near the ruins; a mysterious figure carrying a lantern, a coach drawn by two horses that disappeared into a reservoir without even a ripple and a white horse with red trappings are all on record. Perhaps there is something in this ley line theory after all!

Haymarket Theatre

There are a vast number of theatres across this sceptred isle, a fair-sized percentage are reputedly haunted. Why this should be so, one may only surmise; could it be the collective emotions stirred during a dramatic scene somehow evoking a dormant entity? Are the thespians so beloved of their environment they are unable to take a final bow of mortality?

There are some theatre ghosts whom it is hoped will appear. One fine example is the 'Man in Grey' who inhabits the Theatre Royal in London's Covent Garden. Apparently his appearances are only during the day. He appears quite solid, wears a tricorn hat over a powdered wig and a long grey riding cloak.

He is said only to appear if a production will enjoy a long and successful run. In 1939 during rehearsals for *The Dancing Years*, half the cast saw the apparition. In the 1960s during the successful *The Four Musketeers*, a musical version of Alexander Dumas's classic tale, he appeared

THE CLOCK TOWER, LEICESTER.

The old Haymarket, once a busy area of fine shops, pubs and hotels.

A ghostly drunk is said to stagger down these steps.

several times. The entire cast apparently glimpsed him during a matinée performance, including the late comedian Harry Secombe. Not to be ruffled, Harry later quipped, 'He would always pop up before six, haunting to rule, I suppose.'

The Haymarket has nothing like the Man in Grey but there seems to be something strange about the place. The theatre is quite a recent building, constructed in 1973 as part of the Haymarket redevelopment project, a disappointing structure of grey concrete with a shopping mall, multistorey car park and sundry offices. Many locals still think of the project as 'the day the heart was torn out of the city'.

Probably the most active of the ghosts is a small boy dressed in a Victorian-era sailor suit who tends to be found mostly around the fly tower. During a run of *Joseph and his Amazing Technicolour Dreamcoat* one of the senior backstage staff supervisors had to work late after the production. The supervisor was disturbed from her work by noticing a boy moving from a props basket to the door onto the stage. With all the children involved in the play, the supervisor assumed him to be a member of the cast. He was then told, in no uncertain terms, that he should not be backstage and to leave. This he did by vanishing into nothing.

The ghostly child has also been known to stand at the side of the stage and vanish if approached. Occasionally persons at the side of the stage have felt punches on their upper leg not unlike a child with a tantrum trying to get attention. He is thought to be responsible for major disruption during another musical. During an interval, the musicians left the orchestra pit that was locked behind them. When they returned a scene of total disarray greeted them, several instruments were knocked over and sheets of music were thrown everywhere.

Shortly after the theatre opened, a severe storm and strong winds caused a number of glass panes to fall out in the roof space. At 7.00 a.m. the next morning, the theatre carpenter arrived to begin repairing the damage. In order to reach the roof space he had a hazardous climb of 70ft above the stage. On his arrival at the summit, the carpenter glanced over at a well-dressed young lady. Baffled, the carpenter then got on a gantry to see who the lady was and what she was doing up in such a dangerous area. Then she was gone. The confused carpenter then laboriously descended the ladder. Once down he asked the cleaner if she had let anyone in or had seen anyone apart from himself. He was assured there was nobody else apart from themselves in the locked building.

In early October 2000, during preparation for a production of *The Crucible*, the construction workshop manager was alone in the theatre working well into the early hours of the morning. He watched with interest the darkish figure walking over to stage left. He called over but the figure paid no attention whatsoever. He got up and went over but the figure seemed to melt into the shadows on his approach; the workshop manager was then left to make sense of where the figure had gone — he never did.

Much of the area now occupied by the theatre used to be the horse repository and the George Hotel. There are two accounts that might explain the ghost child. One version is that a small boy fell down a deep well and drowned, the other that a lad was crushed by a wayward barrelful of beer. There were also a multitude of alehouses around the area that may explain the most colourful of the supposed ghosts, a Freddie Frinton-type character. This one would indeed be a sight to behold. It is a drunken man staggering then half falling down the stairs from the theatre reception area. Apparently he clutches a hotel key on a large brass fob. The present author is not alone in thinking of far worse ways to spend eternity, permanently drunk with no hangover to worry about!

Goldsmith Music Library

At the bottom of Belvoir Street, next to the Central Library stands a building that for many years was owned by Sir Herbert Marshall. A known lover of music and a keen pianist, Sir Herbert ran a music emporium and had a piano salon on the first floor. It would be befitting that after his death the building would eventually house the Goldsmith Music Library.

Rumours began to circulate that an unearthly presence was occupying the area where the piano salon used to be. One evening a cleaner saw a previously locked door slowly open of its own volition. If this was not odd enough, the weird chill in the air that had manifested was definitely out of this world. The cleaner tore down the stairs in record time.

On the night of 8 March 1977, a young man was locked inside the building alone to raise funds for a national charity. Apparently all remained quiet until around 3.00 a.m. when the man was awoken by the sounds of stout footsteps moving in close proximity to the camp bed he was lying on. He stared into the darkness absolutely terrified, then he sensed someone close by but he was unwilling to look. A weight was then felt, as if someone was actually sitting on his camp bed. The poor man was frozen with fear and remained so until his unseen companion departed. The brave chap somehow fulfilled his obligation to the sponsorship and it was with much relief that he was let out at 7.00 a.m.

Three years later at nearly 10.00 p.m. several people in an adjacent building heard piano music emanating from somewhere. They listened carefully and tracked the sound to be coming from the music library that was later confirmed to be locked and empty.

The old music library where one may still hear 'haunting melodies'.

Many are convinced that the ghost of Sir Herbert Marshall returns in visitation to his beloved music emporium.

There is a tradition that if one stands next to the granite pillar at the Belvoir Street/Market Street corner entrance to Fenwick's department store, then remains very quiet and patient, one may be rewarded with snatches of pianoforte drifting over on the breeze. This brings a whole new meaning to the term 'haunting melodies' does it not?

St Margaret's Vicarage

There was said to be a ghost residing at the vicarage adjacent to St Margaret's Church. The vicarage has long since made way for a pedestrian subway scheme under Burleys Way.

The canon, Eric Ducker, and the verger, Ernest Morris, who both resided at the vicarage, claimed to have seen the ghost on many occasions. Even after works were carried out to divide the large building into two houses the silent figure continued to carry out its regular perambulations and merely walked through the dividing wall.

A Mrs Gregory who resided at the vicarage for thirty years had no fear of the mysterious visitor. In fact she found it quite fascinating. She also mentioned that for much of the time the ghost would remain inactive but at times of crisis would periodically cause mayhem around the building. Apparently during the two world wars there was much activity: doors would slam violently, one particular incumbent had a door slammed in his face on two occasions, lights would be switched on and off of their own volition, items of furniture would be tipped over, there were unexplained muttering sounds and mysterious disappearances of silver objects or small items that contained the colour red. These were never recovered.

Left: *St Margaret's Church, the old vicarage was adjacent to the churchyard.*

Below: *Municipal Square and Town Hall where Martha still turns up for work.*

At one point during the Second World War, the building was used by fire-watchers. One evening, a watcher, an ex-commando, was so badly affected by an encounter with something that he flatly refused to enter the building ever again.

Among the witnesses to the apparition were an organist and a police constable. The figure was very tall and dressed in dark clothing similar to a cleric. It is thought he was a former vicar but bore no resemblance to any previous occupier.

After the demolition of the vicarage in the late 1960s there were a series of unexplained happenings in the church itself. There were strange cold areas, the bells were heard to peal despite the bell room being empty and locked, and a rigid lampshade shattered although the light bulb was undamaged.

The last known oddity occurred in 1997. A photographer from the *Leicester Mail* was in the churchyard taking photographs of the tomb of one Lord Andrew Rollo. For no apparent reason his camera started malfunctioning then unintelligible words kept forming in the digital time, day and date readout. The photographer was totally at a loss to explain it.

Town Hall

The Municipal Square is an oasis for the tired shopper to rest his weary bones, the office worker to have his lunch in pleasant surroundings or just somewhere to 'flop down'. Not an inch of grass will be visible on summer afternoons. One may be lulled into a restful doze by the winged, bronze lions spitting water into the magnificent fountain. Generations of children have gazed into the fountain at the coins thrown in and have got their heads stuck in the railings (including the present author) then have fallen in whilst trying to reach the money.

The Town Hall itself is a symbol of the city. Built in the style of the Queen Anne period, the building has a few interesting quirks. On the lower frontage there is a duck to welcome the dawn while an owl glares impassively to represent the dusk. The huge clock tower is relied on by many locals and rarely falters. One may set one's watch by it.

Martha is a mystery. This tantalisingly aloof phantom is the shade of a woman once engaged in clerical work at the clock tower end of the building. Apparently Martha died suddenly at home but reported for work the next morning. Nowadays she is rarely seen but often heard. She enjoys 'flexitime' as she is heard outside of normal office hours wandering the echoing corridors. Most of the staff know of Martha and leave it at that.

Perhaps if you idly sit in Municipal Square late on a summer evening when the cleaners have left and gaze at the Town Hall windows, you might just catch a rare glimpse of the elusive Martha working overtime.

Welford Road Cemetery

One would have thought cemeteries to be the last place where ghosts would linger, a place of eternal rest after a lifetime of toil and sorrow. Certainly unlikely a place for evil deeds, mystery, murder and mayhem that are the usual criteria for supposed haunting phenomena. There is an idea, however, that those of a defiant nature will remain earthbound and stay by their earthly remains. There have been some very peculiar occurrences in such places.

Highgate Cemetery in London is well known for constant sightings of mysterious figures that vanish when approached. During the early 1970s there were rumours of some kind of vampire here. Several foxes died violently, a man was found dying after repeatedly stabbing himself in the chest and one visitor discovered a freshly dug-up corpse slumped in his car. One entity in particular, a tall black figure, is said to emanate pure evil. At Mount Carmel Cemetery in Illinois, USA, a most bizarre affair was recorded. In 1921, Julia Buccola died in childbirth aged twenty-nine. For years afterwards, her mother endured dream visitations from Julia in which it was expressed that her body be exhumed. After much persuasion with police and cemetery authorities the morbid task was carried out. To everyone's amazement, Julia's body was in a state of perfect preservation: after six years no decomposition had occurred. The visits ceased, Julia had got the message over that she was okay. Nearby at Resurrection Cemetery an even more bizarre incident occurred in 1976. A man passing by saw a distressed young girl behind the large, iron gates. He told her to calm down and that he would get help. Police arrived to find no young girl but two of the thick iron railings had been bent back. Not only was this odd but the iron was hot and there were imprints of fingers as if the metal was softened to the texture of toffee. Even more strange were the fingerprints in the twisted iron.

Welford Road Cemetery was created in 1855. A William Biggs purchased 17 acres of land on Knighton Hill. Later, the borough took over and created a cemetery that was half-consecrated for Anglicans and half-unconsecrated for the rest. By 1870 more land was needed. Compulsory purchase of a brickworks nearby brought the overall land cover to 30 acres. The cemetery, now full, has 213,000 bodies interred in 40,000 graves.

Unique in its winding paths, the place is a haven for wildlife, with rabbits and foxes a common sight. Many of the tombs have seen better days and parts of the cemetery have an abandoned, eerie feel about it. Recently it has been considered necessary to lay a vast number of stones as a safety measure, this adds to the feel of neglect. At one time there used to be claims of weird lights in the cemetery but this was merely igniting gases or 'will-o'-the-wisp' as it is better known.

Jovan Ugranic who lived nearby would sometimes sit on a bench at the south end on the high ground as it offers excellent views over the city, a tranquil spot to watch a summer sunset. On this one occasion, Jovan nodded off. He awoke in pitch black to an unnatural chill in the June air. It had been one of those sticky, humid days and he felt quite cold. As he stretched he felt a malevolent presence forming close by. Then a feeling of pure dread filled the air. Jovan felt quite uneasy, he looked around but could make out nothing in the gloom. He stood up and began a somewhat rapid jaunt along the path to the gatehouse on University Road. He had the feeling of 'something' staying with him. He knew it was well past the time he should have left and wonders if this was what had caused the unrest. He was glad to get out.

Towards dusk in November 1987 a man was just about to leave a family grave when he felt he was being watched. He jerked around and just saw a fading figure of a tallish person a few feet away. This had a terrible effect on the witness, who refused to go back for many years.

It is not known if the following incident is connected to the cemetery or the old lunatic asylum that used to be opposite on University Road. It was late at night as a car with three occupants swerved violently to avoid someone who appeared in the road. The driver was convinced he had run over the person. In shock, they climbed out expecting the worst, but there was no one anywhere. Relived but baffled they got back in and reported the matter at Charles Street Police Station. The duty sergeant asked the driver if he had been drinking but seemed satisfied when told no. Yet another mystery we will never be able to answer.

six

IN SUBURBIA

The Black Dog

In 1986, three houses on Red House Road were affected by bizarre goings on. In one house the clocks would all stop at the same time, next door had a sixteenth-century looking man regularly appearing in the living room and one of the occupants of the third was so scared by what she saw by the bedroom door that she fell out of the window, spending several weeks in a wheelchair as a result.

It later transpired that the houses were on the site of a coaching inn on Lutterworth Road. Many coaching inns seem to be the scene for haunting phenomena. With so much history and unsavoury characters – highwaymen, vagabonds, murderers and other wretches – perhaps it is not so surprising.

The Black Dog Inn on the London Road in Oadby used to be a little coaching inn. It has had a high number of landlords, thirty-two in all. Richard Ludlam took the inn in 1750 until his death in 1776 when his widow carried it on. Then a William Murton presided. A John Cockam who had a maltings nearby ran the inn for a while. Of all the licensees at the Black Dog, a character called Otho Juba was indeed the most colourful, a total rogue. Juba, a descendant of the slave trade, held the licence for thirteen years which in itself must be quite a feat with some of his activities: selling ale out of hours, giving short measures of spirits and basically turning the inn into a house of ill repute. He was also a known poacher. After many brushes with the law and numerous prosecutions, he was given notice to quit in 1875.

In 1897 the inn was purchased by Lichfield's City Brewery, they were then bought out twenty years later by Wolverhampton and Dudley Breweries. Today the Black Dog is a Banks's house.

The present hosts, Norman and Maureen Green, have had a fairly untroubled period of tenure, up to now. A mysterious presence has come and gone here over many years. As with so many alleged hauntings, the identity of the phantom remains a mystery. There are two likely candidates. A young man was decapitated in the 1950s when his motorcycle ploughed into the inn; is it this mournful shade that lingers on? The other possibility is that the ghost is one James Hawker, a villainous and evil man with no shame. He was undoubtedly a regular at the inn and after one of his drunken binges he was seen no more. His body was discovered nearby under mysterious circumstances. This might have had something to do with his poaching exploits. Defiant to the end, Hawker's gravestone carries the epitaph: 'I will poach 'til I die'.

The old stables is now a skittle alley but was used as a mortuary for a few years which has, of course, boosted the rumours of ghostly goings on. There is evidence of a bricked-up entrance in the cellar that is said to be a secret tunnel and adds to the cornucopia of mystery and intrigue.

Norman has only experienced two minor unexplained incidents, both of which were connected to the cellar. One evening, Norman was behind the bar pulling a pint of ale when the flow slowly petered out to just a trickle. With just a hint of colourful language, Norman

The Black Dog, an ancient inn with a mysterious presence.

laboriously went down the cellar to see what was wrong. He discovered the gas cylinder turnkey had been tampered with. It was almost in the off position. This made no sense at all as Norman himself had switched the thing on at opening up time. If he had forgotten to do it there would have been no pressure throughout the period of opening the pub. On a later occasion, Norman was setting a barrel when all of a sudden the hosepipe used for rinsing down the thralls began to snake about. Completely puzzled, Norman examined the hosepipe, found nothing to explain it and carried on his cellar work.

I paid a visit to the Black Dog one evening a while ago. I had along a young lady who is more attuned to ghostly effects than most. After a convivial beer or three, Norman, the young lady and I visited the cellar. After a while the young lady 'got' a young boy of around six to eight years old, very scruffy with hobnail boots; she 'felt' his name began with the letter 'S'. She claimed that he liked to play in the cellar and that he was fond of Norman. She added that he was less than keen about me. In the skittle alley there was the ghost of a young stable lad. He was about fourteen years of age, he had a brownish waistcoat, jodhpurs and riding boots, his name was Bill and he was in visitation, like an atmospheric return. Interestingly, the young lady picked up on nothing at all in an area of the pub where a customer claimed to have seen a darkish form materialise then slowly disappear.

The young lady returned with some friends a few weeks later. After darkness set in they went to the skittle alley, as it was not in use. They arranged some chairs into a circle then sat quietly in the dark to see if anything might occur. After nearly an hour they decided they had had enough, just then one of the group jolted. He claimed he had been struck on the leg by a small missile, possibly a stone. It seemed to have come from the far end of the alley. When the lights were switched on there was no stone or anything else in evidence.

Maureen has not experienced anything herself but keeps an open mind on the idea of ghosts. She also does a mean cheese and onion cob (local dialect for bread roll) and is the perfect host. For research purposes, the present author has paid additional visits – the sufferance one has to endure in the name of art!

The Black Dog is an alehouse of the finest tradition with a character all of its own.

Glenfield

This pleasant little spot a few miles west of Leicester seems to be a focus for mysterious characters and supernatural oddities.

In the late 1990s, major renovation work at a property on Main Street may have stirred up something of a ghostly nature.

Some of the workmen were convinced that the place was haunted. The sixteenth-century Grade II-listed pile, the Old Rectory, had been purchased in order for the building to be converted into a number of office units.

It was getting towards the end of the renovation project, when one day a large industrial vacuum cleaner used for the removal of plaster dust and other small debris refused to operate near the staircase for some reason. It simply would not work. One of the workmen, Ady, somewhat perplexed and uttering one or two expletives, gave up with the thing and carried on with another task. A few minutes later the machine spluttered into life. The dazed builder examined the wire and there was no power supply shutdown; he scratched his head and swore again.

His mates would have enjoyed this enormously but one chap, Geoff, got his comeuppance. He had stayed on late one evening and, as he was about to leave, he felt someone pulling at his shirt. He knew he was alone in the building. Frantically, he rushed out.

Arthur Huscroft, who lives nearby, is a ghost expert and dowser. He was invited over by the owners to see what he could make of the claims. After an exhaustive six-hour evaluation of the entire property, Arthur revealed his findings. There seemed to be several 'energy sources', the most notable areas being around the hallway and lower staircase. Elsewhere in the building there were two places where olfactory sensations in the form of strong lavender were noted; two other persons confirmed this strange phenomenon. Arthur's overall opinion was that there were several harmless spirits in the building. They were less than impressed with the changes to the rectory but would eventually settle down.

The Dominion pub on Glenfield Road is an average-style alehouse and caters for all ages. One or two of the bar staff are reluctant to venture into the cellar in case they meet Bert. Bert is around his mid-thirties, has mousy, grey hair. He wears black trousers, a black open waistcoat and stout black boots. This good-looking fellow has no shirt though, so on occasion he is affectionately known as, 'Bert without a shirt'.

In this vicinity there are many quarries. In the latter part of the eighteenth century a clay pit existed where the pub now stands. Such places were rife with danger and there were many instances of serious injury and sometimes death. There was an explosion at the clay pit in which one man was killed instantly. With Bert's rugged appearance and attire, the ghost is believed to be him.

He appears quite solid and has been mistaken for a builder by those unaware of him. A former barmaid, Sarah Kinton, never saw him but had a nerve-racking experience in the cellar one evening. She had just arrived and heard a rattling sound above the roar of the cellar cooling unit that was quite loud in itself. Sarah slowly went over to the bottle store and peered in. Several shelves were rattling violently. Sarah screamed and tore up the stairs.

The early morning cleaners apparently saw him the most. He would simply appear and disappear in a split second. The women had no fear of Bert. One lady admitted to sometimes greeting him if she felt he was around, 'Morning Bert.' Another cleaner remarked on several instances where doors would open for her, 'I felt he was opening the doors for me, like a gentleman.'

The Knoll

In the leafy suburb of Oadby there are many grand houses, most of which were built in the early 1900s for the successful shoe, hosiery and wool business people. Many of the houses are like small mansions.

One such house stands amid the splendour of the Harold Martin Botanical Gardens, a sprawling oasis of rare horticultural treasures. The house is called The Knoll. It was built in 1907 by brick-maker William Winterton who owned the Newstar Brickworks on Barkby Road. The house is quite unique in that it has small Tudor bricks. In 1784 a brick tax was introduced so it became prudent to use larger bricks as we have today. Of course Mr Winterton would have had no problem with this burden.

We have heard the term 'making a mint' with highly successful business ventures. This would certainly apply to the people that acquired the house several years later, the Fox family. Their confectionery, particularly the unique glacier mint, is as popular today as it was seventy years ago.

The University of Leicester bought the house in 1964, one of many in the area. With the ever-increasing volume of students, it was necessary to provide suitable accommodation not only where it was found to be quiet to aid study but to be near to the university itself. Much conversion work would be undertaken to create dormitories, study areas, kitchens and dining facilities, these houses and various facilities are collectively known as halls of residence.

The Knoll, a possible past tragedy may have left psychic torment behind.

Among the staff required with the residences' smooth running will be the sub-warden. He plays a vital role in that he will be the first contact with any queries or problems that may arise. The sub-warden lives in and is always on call during term time. A massive sigh of relief must be given at the onset of the three long vacation periods, Christmas, Easter and the three-month-long summer break. Peace at last!

A mixed blessing though for the sub-warden of The Knoll. Anywhere that has had a lot going on then is suddenly devoid of people will feel quiet and lonely; at The knoll it may feel quiet but not lonely. There is an occupant from the past to keep the sub-warden company.

One former sub-warden, who I will call Alan, was initially sceptical of claims of some form of spiritual activity in the place but became less cynical during the five years he lived there. He heard several accounts from students of which he made careful notes: Growling sounds emanating from the speakers of a stereo unit while the machine was switched off, rattling sounds from a fireplace, a radio-controlled model car that apparently whirred into action momentarily despite there being no batteries in the control unit and, most oddly, a student who was in a small dormitory who claimed to see a shape coming up behind him reflected in a mirror, yet when he looked around there was no one there.

Alan showed me a photograph, one of several taken during a social event in the main hall. On this exposure there appears to be a misty form of a man astride a horse. The normally sceptical Alan watched me analysing the image and piped up, 'If that's cigarette smoke I'm a Chinaman.'

The heart-shaped pond where the cause of the unrest is said to have originated.

Many such photographs have come to light. Our normal field of vision of the light spectrum is 390–780 nanometres from violet to red. Still and video cameras go beyond these limits to near infra-red. The camera 'sees' what the naked eye fails to observe. Let us not forget though the possibility of lens aberration, light reflections, moisture or other simple explanations. Such ambiguous photographs are occasionally thought-provoking but usually merely entertaining.

Cleaners Janet and Malveen both claim to have sensed a strange feeling on the first floor. Janet described one incident where she felt a static charge passing through her and fine cobweb-like brushes on her face. One cleaner reportedly left after seeing a young girl wearing a long nightdress looking over the landing balustrade. At the time, the hall was sectioned to just male students so she asked what she was doing there. The girl vanished.

There is no known record of a murder here or any violent death that tends to be the usual reason for haunting phenomena of this kind. There is, however, a story of an incident outside in the grounds at the heart-shaped pond. Apparently a young girl looking out of the window in one of the rooms on the first floor saw a man lurking near the pond. She went outside then saw a body floating in the pond. It was not the man she had seen. The girl was so traumatised by what she had witnessed, that she became psychologically disturbed. Nothing was ever mentioned about the alleged body. Had she imagined it or even looked upon a ghostly vision of the past?

The Marquis Wellington, London Road

Another pub that is near to where a gallows once stood is the Marquis Wellington. The pub was built in 1813 in an area then known as Gallows Hill. The gallows itself was situated a few hundred yards east from the London Road/Evington Road junction. The obligatory 'last meal' of a jug of ale to lessen the fears of being strung-up went on here.

The elusive ghost prefers to remain quiet for years then suddenly act up for a few days before lying dormant yet again.

In 1982, hosts Les and Andrea Pike incurred the wrath of the mysterious phantom. Fred, as he was dubbed, began his tirade by constantly ringing the doorbell at exactly 3.00 a.m. on many occasions. Running a pub is tiring enough without nocturnal upheaval such as this. Les checked by looking down from the bedroom window on most of the occasions to see no one at the door. Glasses flew off shelves, several plants were hurled across the bar and the cash register would suddenly operate by itself. Towards the end of his antics, Fred demonstrated his musical prowess by tinkling the ivories on an old upright piano up in the attic. The fact that most of the wires had broken made no difference.

The one incident that shook Les happened late one night after closing time. He had to go down to the cellar to put some ale back through the filters. When a new barrel is started one has to 'pull off' a bucket or two of ale from the pipes, this is then returned to the barrel after service. Les got to the bottom of the stairs, turned and almost bumped into a man wearing eighteenth-century-type clothing. As Les was looking down he saw his feet and legs first and noted the man had buckled shoes. Les tore upstairs in total shock. The beer could wait.

A Mr Humphries took over the pub in 1985. All was quiet for a year or two then Charlie, as he was now known, rattled his chains for a few months. This time there was less

Marquis Wellington, a busy alehouse with a mischievous ghost.

upheaval, the odd glass thrown, doors opening on their own and a chill presence. The pub dog, Tuppence, would react oddly and bark at the cellar door and, ironically, the spirit store. The pub was altered in the mid-1990s. Structural change, as well as 'bringing on' ghostly disturbances, can also have an arresting effect that may be the case here, as the present landlord has nothing to report.

Thorncroft

Those who are keen on travel will be familiar with the name Thomas Cook. In 1841, Cook arranged a railway excursion for the Temperance Society from Leicester to Loughborough. It was a huge success and further travel excursions became very popular – the rest, as they say, is history.

Cook provided for his family very well indeed. Thorncroft, a very elegant house, was built in 1887 on London Road.

It was a happy house. Thomas Cook's daughter, Annie Elizabeth, grew very attracted to the handsome features of Mr Higgins, a clerk in her father's travel business. Mr Higgins was a regular visitor to the house and the attraction was mutual. It was only a matter of time before the young couple fell in love.

The relationship flourished and with much excitement the pair declared their wish to marry. The family were furious, particularly her brother who had little time for her intended. Not only was it not the done thing for family and business affairs to become entangled but Mr Higgins was considered to be totally unsuitable. With the strict Victorian values of the time such a marriage could not proceed.

Thomas Cook: travel pioneer and strict disciplinarian.

A few days later, Annie Elizabeth was found still and cold in the bathtub. It was later established that carbon monoxide fumes were emanating from a faulty gas boiler in the bathroom. Whatever the cause, Annie Elizabeth was dead.

Today the building is a regional headquarters for a national charity. Volunteers are used to the odd, chill breezes near the top of the staircase, the unexplained footsteps along the corridor and the shadow that flits from the bathroom to the stairs.

Did Annie Elizabeth die of a broken heart, committing suicide by drowning herself, or was her untimely death a result of poisonous fumes? We will never know, but without doubt, this pitiful wraith remains in the house and is unable to rest.

A Haunted Hotel

If Mike Brearey knew what his actions might have stirred up, he would have kept well away from that attic room. Mike and his wife had recently taken the position as hosts at one of the larger commercial hotels on London Road. On a wet Sunday afternoon in the autumn of 1993, Mike thought to clear out the attic. He had earlier been up to inspect the room as a slight damp patch on the top floor wall had appeared, but although there had been recent heavy rain he found no leaks in the roof.

The job took around an hour. There was not a huge amount of junk and nothing of any value amongst the spider-infested floor beams. There were some old clothes, old tins, a broken gas lamp and a few books, a collection of recipes cut from French newspapers and other bits and bobs. Mike dropped the two full bin liners through the hatch and as he was about to leave he noticed a faded brown envelope pinned to the timber upright. He pulled it away and put the envelope into his overalls pocket.

A week later, another Sunday afternoon, Mike decided to inspect some of the rooms as he had taken on two new chambermaids and wished to see if their work was up to scratch. As he approached room 12, he sensed someone behind him. Mike looked around to see no one then a male voice uttered, 'Again'. Then stifled laughter was heard. Mike came away completely terrified. A stout Yorkshireman, running from a 'voice' – surely there was no such things as ghosts; he was working too hard, imagining things.

A few weeks later, a guest who was a traveller and often stayed overnight, told Mike over breakfast that his room, number 12, felt freezing cold and clammy. Later in the day Mike went up to see if the heating was in order. As he unlocked the door and turned the handle, Mike was horrified to see the key quickly turn around and re-lock. Mike fled. He told his wife who, on being reminded of the supposed ghost, passed over the envelope found in his overalls prior to putting them in with the washing earlier. Inside was a faded photograph of a young man wearing a mackintosh and trilby-type hat.

Over the next few months there were various minor incidents that defied rational explanation including an electric kettle boiling whilst unplugged and a white shirt 'levitating'. Mike accepted there was indeed a ghost abroad. He dubbed it 'Fred'. Mike decided to look into the whole subject of ghosts and obtained a few books. After studying a number of case histories, he concluded there were several avenues to go down. Mike decided to become actively involved in researching the matter rather then merely just being a 'victim'.

A bit of detective work was needed. The house was built for private residence in 1904. From 1930 it was a school. Later several physicians occupied the premises. The unrest had first come

Just who was the man in the photograph?

to light after the attic clearout, was the photograph a lead? Who was the man in the picture? Was there a connection to room 12? There were more questions than answers. There was also a hotel to run. Help was needed.

After a long period of consultations it came to light that for a short period during the Second World War the building was used by the military as a hospital for servicemen. Also, there were various detachments of both British and American servicemen on nearby Victoria Park and it would have been commonplace to take over large buildings in the area as temporary headquarters for covert operations.

By June 1994 the mysterious un-paying guest had seemingly checked out. Mike and his wife were relieved as running a hotel was stressful enough without having to cope with such bizarre incidents that made no sense.

In some ways, Mike missed Fred. He wrote a document of the affair, 'Fred the Friendly Ghost'. He was glad he had thought to study the subject as it had helped enormously. He had gleaned that in similar cases the disturbances are simply to get attention, to get things done. Perhaps Fred was happy now, his questions answered.

It was later revealed that an American airman who was tended by one of the nurses, to whom he became very fond, was killed in active service. Perhaps this was the man in the photograph and he had come back to find her. Could room 12 have been the nurse's quarters?

Other local titles published by Tempus

Central Leicester
STEPHEN BUTT

Despite the city's motto (*semper eadem*, 'Always the Same') Leicester has witnessed great changes over the last 150 years. This fascinating collection of over 200 photographs is a pictorial history of this period of Leicester's history. This book navigates the old town, with detailed and informative captions describing buildings, shops, pubs and transport.

0 7524 3674 0

Leicester Voices
CYNTHIA BROWN

These personal memories of the past provide a valuable record of what life used to be like in Leicester. Each story illustrates a different aspect of life in the city as it once was. From memories of childhood and schooldays, work and family, war and peace, each piece offers an oral testimony into the lives of people who have lived in and known Leicester over the decades.

0 7524 2657 5

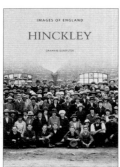

Hinckley
GRAHAM KEMPSTER

The life and times of Hinckley over more than a century are illustrated in this collection of old photographs selected from the archives of the *Hinckley Times*. Young Hinckley people and recent arrivals to the town will be amazed to see familiar streets in the unfamiliar settings of days gone by and older residents will enjoy the nostalgia as they are reminded of them as they once were.

0 7524 3619 8

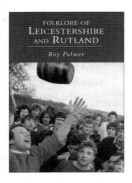

Folklore of Leicestershire and Rutland
ROY PALMER

This book is a comprehensive survey, drawing on a wide range of printed, manuscript and oral material. The topics covered include local legend and lore, ghosts and witchcraft, folk medicine, work and play, sport and fairs, crime and punishment, music, drama and calendar customs in the counties of Leicestershire and Rutland. Roy Palmer is a long-standing member of the English Folk Dance and Song Society and the Folklore Society.

0 7524 2468 8

If you are interested in purchasing other books published by Tempus, or in case you have difficulty finding any Tempus books in your local bookshop, you can also place orders directly through our website

www.tempus-publishing.com